ENTER CERTAIN PLAYERS

Hilton Edwards and Micheál Mac Liammóir. Photograph by Paul Joyce © 1977.

EDITED BY PETER LUKE

ENTER CERTAIN PLAYERS

EDWARDS - MAC LIAMMOIR AND THE GATE
1928-1978

THE DOLMEN PRESS

Set in Baskerville type with Othello display
and printed and published in the Republic of Ireland
at the Dolmen Press
North Richmond Industrial Estate, North Richmond Street, Dublin 1

Designed by Liam Miller

Published in October 1978

ISBN 0 85105 345 9 paper covered
    0 85105 346 7 bound

Distributed in North America by
Humanities Press Inc., 171 First Avenue, Atlantic Highlands, New Jersey 07716

Acknowledgement is made to An Chomhairle Ealaíon (The Arts Council of Ireland) for their assistance in producing this book, published to mark the Golden Jubilee of Edwards – Mac Liammóir Dublin Gate Theatre Productions Limited.

CONTENTS

ILLUSTRATIONS

PETER LUKE
playwright, short-story writer, member of the board of directors of
the Dublin Gate Theatre

The first purpose of this Festschrift is to pay homage to two men, Hilton Edwards and Micheál Mac Liammóir, on this the fiftieth anniversary of their theatrical partnership. The second is to record for posterity the life-work of this supremely and diversely talented pair, whose corpus of achievement is central to the theatrical history of Ireland.

Alas, between the concept and completion of this volume, one of the partners died. On 6 March 1978 Micheál Mac Liammóir, tired perhaps of a body that no longer served his active and creative mind, relinquished hold on this life. Two days afterwards the whole of Dublin, it seemed, came out into the streets to see its much-loved maestro passing to his rest. When on its way from the University Church in St. Stephen's Green to the hill of Howth, the funeral cortege came to Harcourt Terrace, it paused for a moment outside No. 4. This was the house that had been the birthplace of a thousand dreams and schemes that came to be realised in one form or another on the stage of the Gate Theatre. Since that day, at the request of sympathetic neighbours, and with the unanimous agreement of the Dublin Corporation, the little terrace known to so many famous theatrical people, and to many others besides, has been re-named Mac Liammóir Terrace.

On the day Micheál Mac Liammóir died, the other maestro, Hilton Edwards, true to the old theatre maxim that 'the show must go on', decided that their Golden Jubilee should even so be celebrated and that this book should go through the press. And now here it is to hand: a volume with seventeen essays concerning the two heroes and the theatre they created, written by as many distinguished writers of, and on, the theatre; together with a full chronology of the *œuvre* of the Dublin Gate, a bibliography of the written work of Edwards and Mac Liammóir, and numerous illustrations relating to their joint accomplishment.

As editor of *Enter Certain Players* I would like here to record my gratitude to many people who have in so many different ways helped towards the celebration of the Edwards - Mac Liammóir Golden Jubilee. In particular I wish to thank Mr. Colm O Briain and An Chomhairle Ealaíon (The Arts Council), without whose assistance the publication of this Festschrift would not have been possible. Nor, indeed, could its publication have been achieved without the contributions made by so many distinguished writers and scholars whose essays appear between these covers. To them my most grateful thanks. I also wish to acknowledge the kindness of the Department of Foreign Affairs and the editor of *Ireland Today* for permission to reproduce an article by Mr. Desmond Rushe. No small part of the Jubilee celebrations depends on gifts and loans of drawings, pictures and other memorabilia. Many of these will be seen in the *All For Hecuba* Exhibition at the Hugh Lane Municipal Gallery and some of them have been reproduced in this book. My sincere thanks to their many donors and loaners.

Two people in particular deserve more than the mere thanks that I can give them. The first is Mr. Liam Miller whose enthusiasm for this project, whose skill as a publisher and whose impeccable taste as a designer, has given us this handsome volume. And, lastly, my warmest thanks go to Miss Patricia Turner, the Gate archivist, who has not only been responsible for the chronology and bibliography of this book, but who has cheerfully given uncounted hours of her own time in helping Liam Miller and myself towards its publication.

8

Cover design for *All for Hecuba* by Micheál Mac Liammóir.
This design is used for the poster of the Jubilee Exhibition, 1978.

JAMES MASON

I drink to the health of Hilton & Michael. Thus too I celebrate the Golden Jubilee of their Life's work at the Gate. It could be said that I am a constant celebrant since these two were my masters & I carry with pride, the wrinkles that were imprinted during that happy year when I was attempting to measure up to their standards. I wish them long & happy lives!

James Mason

Of the many players who first learned their craft on the boards of the Gate Theatre James Mason is today certainly one of the most distinguished. His tribute to the joint anniversary came only days before the death of Micheál Mac Liammóir. (Ed.)

THE DUBLIN GATE THEATRE

The Rotunda buildings, 1785, from James Malton's aquatint, 1795.
The theatre occupies the central building with the pillared portico.

The New Rooms

In 1785 an elegant suite of rooms were begun to be added to the Rotunda, and the Rotunda itself to be much beautified in its external appearance, by Mr. RICHARD JOHNSTON, Architect, assisted by FREDERICK TRENCH, Esq. to whose exertions and taste in architecture these buildings are much indebted. The foundation stone of the New Rooms was laid by the Duke of RUTLAND, the 17th of July, 1785. The Tympan of the pediment in the centre is adorned with his arms, encircled by the collar of the garter, and other ornaments. The New Rooms form a pleasing range of buildings, 101 feet in extent, parrallel with Cavendish-row, the east side of the Square.

*   *   *

The New Rooms are superb; they consist of two principal apartments, one over the other, 86 feet long, by 40 broad; the lower is the Ball, the upper is the Supper and Tea Room. There is a smaller Ball Room on the ground floor, 60 feet by 24, which also serves as a room for refreshments when the larger is occupied. The upper room is very elegently enriched : between pilasters against the walls are trophies, where shields of cut glass, and other glittering ornaments, have a very brilliant appearance : there are several lesser rooms for cards and refreshments. Besides weekly concerts in the winter season, there are here held subscription balls, supported by the first nobility and gentry; card assemblies; and every season, a masquerade or two. The entertainments of the Rotunda, during the winter, form the most elegant amusements of Dublin; it is opened every Sunday evening, in summer, for the purpose of a promenade, when tea and coffee are given in the superb upper room. The receipts of the whole, after defraying the incidental expenses, go to the support of the Hospital.

from *A Picturesque and Descriptive View
of the City of Dublin* by James Malton, 1799

THE DUBLIN GATE THEATRE 1928-1978

Robert Hogan

Michael Scott

Brian Friel

John Finegan

Terence de Vere White

Séamus Kelly

Mary Manning

Gabriel Fallon

John Jordan

Denis Johnston

Christine Longford

Hilton Edwards and
Micheál Mac Liammóir
outside the Gate theatre.

Micheál Mac Liammóir in *The Marriage of Saint Francis*, 1935.

The Comedy of Errors by William Shakespeare, 1938.

ROBERT HOGAN
professor of English at the University of Delaware

13 On Saturday, 15 September 1928, a number of Dublin citizens received in the mail a brief four-page circular from an organization called 'The Dublin Gate Theatre Studio'. The Studio's address was the Peacock Theatre, and its directors were listed as Hilton Edwards, Micheál Mac Liammóir, Georóid O Lochlainn, and D. Bannard Cogley. The circular announced the first season of this new theatre group, and featured the now-familiar black and white drawing of a semi-naked male figure bathed in a glare of stage lights and heroically pushing open the gates of tragedy and comedy. The announcement itself read:

> It is proposed to open the Dublin Gate Theatre Studio in October, 1928, for the production of modern and progressive plays, unfettered by theatrical convention. The London Gate Theatre has been extraordinarily successful, and the directors of the Dublin Gate Theatre are in a position to avail themselves of this organisation for procuring plays that would not otherwise be within the reach of Dublin Theatrical circles.
>
> It is intended eventually to run the Dublin Gate Theatre Studio as a private theatre, and as soon as there are sufficient numbers, the Studio will be exclusively for these and their friends.
>
> It is proposed to produce a play every fortnight. Produced upon a Sunday night, each play will run for twelve nights. There will be a performance each Sunday, but there will be no performance on Thursdays and no matinee.
>
> It is hoped to hold from time to time lectures, discussions, and exhibitions of painting for the benefit of members.
>
> In addition to its Continental repertoire the Dublin Gate Theatre Studio is prepared to consider with a view to production all plays of a suitable nature submitted. The Studio will utilise as much Dublin talent as possible. Engagements will be conducted upon a professional basis.
>
> It is not the intention of the studio to encroach upon the activities of any existing Dublin theatrical organisation; rather it is the desire of the Gate to introduce a new element, both in the play and its production.

The first season of plays was to be selected from the following rather astonishing group: *Nju* by Ossip Dymov, *The Adding Machine* by Jean Cocteau (!), *Orphée* by Cocteau, *Gas* and *Kolportage* by Kaiser, *The Hairy Ape* and *All God's Chillun Got Wings* by O'Neill, *Hobbleman* by Toller, *Brand*, *Peer Gynt*, and *Hedda Gabler* by Ibsen, *Simoon* by Strindberg, *Six Stokers Who Own the Bloomin' Earth* by Elmer Greensfelder, *Jenseits* by Walter Hassenclever [*sic*], *The God of Vengeance* by Sholom Asch, *Rampa* by Max Mohr, *Schweiger* by Franz Werfel, *Le Paquebot Ténacité* by Vildrac, *Theatre of the Soul* and *The Merry*

Death by Evreinov, *Maya* by Simon Gantillon, *The Black Maskers* by Andreyev, *Diarmuid and Gráinne* by Mac Liammóir, *Salomé* by Wilde, *Pelleas and Mélisande* by Maeterlinck, and Goethe's *Faust*.

In 1927 and 1928, the Abbey Theatre had given a nod to the dramatic literature of the world by staging *The Emperor Jones, Oedipus at Colonnus, King Lear* and a piece by the Quinteros, but the staples of the Abbey repertoire remained plays by George Shiels, Lennox Robinson, T. C. Murray, Brinsley MacNamara and, of course, the three popular early pieces of Seán O'Casey. So a list of possible productions, such as the Gate Theatre Studio proposed, was for Dublin a rather dazzling prospect indeed.

Where did this provocative phenomenon spring from? Despite the intense, novel, and influential flurry of theatrical activity in Dublin that began in 1899 with the Irish Literary Theatre and more or less ended a decade later with the death of Synge, Dublin had hardly ever been in the forefront of theatrical experiment. Even what has been called the 'Dramatic Renaissance' was more a naissance than a re-naissance; and, as far as theatrical experiment went, that naissance was more reactionary than *avant garde*. The new Irish dramatic movement looked for its inspiration to the disappearing Irish past, rather than to the Irish political or cultural present or future; and its claim for experimentation was based largely on the quirky individual vision of one man, John Synge. Even the early poetic dramas of Yeats — such as *The Countess Cathleen, Kathleen ni Houlihan, The Shadowy Waters, The Pot of Broth* and the others — seemed influenced more by Maeterlinck or even Stephen Phillips than by anything that could have been called *avant garde*. Around the turn of the century, Frank Fay knew some Ibsen but liked Rostand better, and James Joyce knew both his Ibsen and his Hauptmann, but neither Fay nor Joyce had much influence on what was finally produced. Otherwise Dublin around the turn of the century was simply another provincial city that booked road companies of *The Private Secretary* into the Gaiety and F. Marriot Watson's *The Trail of the Serpent* into the Queen's.

The new Irish drama, then, was basically an ingrown and an inward-looking movement. It and the entire literary movement of the 1890s and after can be to a large extent explained as one of the few possible patriotic reactions left after the political debacle of Parnell's fall. Despite Yeats, it was not a movement much interested in art *per se*, and when Frank Fay looked toward Scandinavia he was more interested in how Ole Bull had founded a repertory theatre than in how Ibsen had written his late plays. Nevertheless, there was one man of the time who was interested, in his own peculiar way, in Ibsen and Strindberg, and this was one of the founders of the Irish Literary Theatre, Edward Martyn.

Some of Martyn's plays, such as *The Bending of the Bough* and *Maeve*, were seen as attempts to do for Ireland what Ibsen had done for Norway. However, this was not quite the case, for Martyn's early plays were much more romantic and mystical and individual than they were realistic depictions of Ireland's contemporary social problems. Martyn, in fact, was too formed, too maimed even, by Ireland ever to become an Irish Ibsen, much less an Irish Strindberg. Nevertheless, within the limitations of his talent and his character, Martyn did try to foster an interest in international theatre. He was involved with Flora MacDonnell and the Players' Club in producing Ibsen, after he had broken with Yeats and Lady Gregory. He encouraged Count Mark-ievicz's Independent Theatre, which produced Galsworthy. And, most significantly, he founded the Theatre of Ireland in Hardwicke Street. The productions of the Theatre of Ireland were usually insufficiently rehearsed and amateurish, but a remarkable group of people took part in them — Thomas and John MacDonagh, Joseph Plunkett, Pádraic Colum, Máire nic Shiubhlaigh, James Stephens, Rutherford Mayne, and even for a while the young Mac Liammóir. The theatre produced some new Irish plays by Martyn, Eimar O'Duffy, Seumas O'Kelly and the MacDonaghs, but its general tone was undoubtedly established by its productions of Ibsen, Chekhov and Strindberg. The Rising disrupted the theatre, and, although it lingered on a few years until Martyn's death, it was never really popular or successful. What it did do, however, was to keep a small Irish window open on the theatre of the world.

In 1918, Yeats, Lennox Robinson, James Stephens and others founded the Dublin Drama League which used the Abbey stage for occasional weekend performances and which used some of the Abbey actors and some of the city's talented amateurs, to present a wide range of world theatre, ranging from Greeks to Pirandello, O'Neill, Lenormand, Toller, Andreyev and Cocteau. The League existed intermittently for ten years. Its productions, although quickly gotten up, tended to be more polished than those of the Irish theatre, and the League's influence was certainly far greater. Seeing Toller performed by the Drama League was, for instance, a revelation to Seán O'Casey.

In 1928, the Drama League closed down, and so the time was ripe and receptive for an international theatre in Dublin, and it was precisely at that moment that two earnest, talented and dedicated young men appeared on the scene.

Hilton Edwards is an Englishman who toured with Charles Doran's Shakespearean company and played with the Old Vic before being hired in 1927 for a tour with Anew McMaster's company in Ireland. There, he met McMaster's brother-in-law, Micheál Mac Liammóir, who was playing with the company, and in 1928 they began their long partnership by producing MacLiammóir's Irish version of *Diarmuid and Gráinne* in Galway. In October of that year, they opened the Dublin Gate Theatre Studio at the Abbey's little Peacock Theatre with an impressive production of *Peer Gynt*. Since then, Edwards has directed more than three hundred plays for the Gate and acted in many of them. His influence on the Irish theatre is well summed up by Mac Liammóir, who wrote:

> It was his arrival on the Irish scene that was the first signal for the searchlights of interest and understanding to be turned, not away from the author, who at the Abbey had been pre-eminent from the beginning even over the actor, but equally upon the director and his art. It was he who introduced to Dublin methods of production, decor, and lighting, handling of mass effects, experiments in choral speaking, in scenic continuity, in symphonic arrangements of incidental music, of mime and gesture, hitherto barely understood. It is impossible to see the work of any of the younger directors without tracing a great portion of its inspiration to him. Production, as it is understood in Dublin today in what I must call the resident companies would undoubtedly exist in one form or another, but it would not be as it is.

Mac Liammóir himself was a fascinating figure who began his career as a child actor in *Peter Pan* and with Beerbohm Tree in *Oliver Twist*. He seemed really a man born out of his times; he should have hobnobbed with Wilde and Beerbohm in the Yellow Nineties, for in many ways he was the last of the dandies. His prose suggests the ornate elegance of Pater, his drawing the feline elegance of Beardsley. His contributions to the Gate were as significant and various as those of his partner. The effect of a typical Gate production — if one could really call any production from such a disparate repertoire typical — derived not only from Edwards's firm and perceptive direction, but also from a sense of taste and style inherent in Mac Liammóir's designs for sets and costumes. As an actor, Mac Liammóir ranked with Cyril Cusack and Siobhán McKenna as the best known outside of Ireland and as among the best within it. As a writer, he gave the theatre witty original scripts and craftsmanlike adaptations, as well as an invaluable series of memoirs and, his last book, the enchanting fictional autobiography entitled *Enter a Goldfish*.

For its first two seasons, the Gate's plays were done in the Abbey's small experimental Peacock Theatre. For the third season, the Gate moved into the Rotunda, where the architect Michael Scott had converted a second-story ballroom into a moderate-sized theatre. The stage was small, there was little room for the storage of sets, and no fly space. Despite these handicaps, the theatre's productions were the most visually exciting to be seen in Dublin.

A pictorial record of the theatre's first seven seasons is preserved in *The Gate Book* whose many photographs attest to the taste and ability of Mac Liammóir as a designer. The photographs make it apparent that the theatre was attempting to develop no one style, but rather to find the appropriate style for each of the widely varied shows that were produced. There were realistic interiors for plays that demanded them— a simple cottage for Mary Manning's *The Happy Family*, a parlour of a Big House for Lady Longford's *Mr. Jiggins of Jigginstown*, a spacious drawing room for *Lady Windermere's Fan*. There were stylized interiors — a whimsical overdecoration for *The Importance of Being Earnest*, an almost Dali-esque amusement park scene for *Liliom*, a child-like agleyness for *Ten Nights in a Bar Room*. Some plays or scenes were merely done in front of painted backcloths—the minute cartoon of the Coliseum for Lady Longford's *Queens and Emperors*, the formal decoration for *A Bride for the Unicorn*, and the suggested interiors for *The Old Lady Says 'No!'*, both by Denis Johnston; each aptly interprets the style and spirit of the play.

For many years, Edwards and Mac Liammóir were able to hold a company together—despite secessions of some remarkable actors, among them the young Orson Welles, Geraldine Fitzgerald, the young Cyril Cusack, James Mason, and Peggy Cummins. Of course, the most telling secession was not by an actor, but by Lord Longford, who was the chairman of the theatre's board and who for several years had footed many of the bills. In 1936, when Edwards, Mac Liammóir, and part of the Gate company were touring in Egypt, they learned to their surprise and dismay that Longford had formed a company which was appearing in England billed as the Gate Theatre. A compromise was eventually worked out whereby the Edwards-Mac Liammóir group kept the name of the Gate, and each company played in the theatre for six months and toured for six.

During the war, tours outside of Ireland were impossible, and Edwards and Mac Liammóir played several seasons at the Gaiety Theatre in Dublin, which had a seating capacity three or four times as large as the Gate. In the early 1960s, the fortunes of the theatre seemed finally to flag, as Edwards became involved in the newly-formed Telefís Eireann, and as Mac Liammóir toured the world in his one-man show *The Importance of Being Oscar*. The financial status of the theatre was always shaky, and for a while it seemed as if the venture might go the way of so many others. However, the Irish government, in a belated but admirable testimony to the value of the theatre, offered sufficient help for the work to proceed. Today, fifty years after its inception, and despite the death of Mac Liammóir, the theatre still bravely holds open the Gates of Comedy and Tragedy.

It seems appropriate, after these fifty years of dedicated endeavour, to ponder what is the real nature of the Gate's achievement. In his book, *The Mantle of Harlequin*, Edwards wrote:

> When the Dublin Gate Theatre was started by my partner, Micheál Mac Liammóir, and myself in the late twenties theatrical revolution was in the air. Just as the Abbey had been swept along on the tide of naturalism, not in itself a native product of the soil, so the Gate bore a more obvious evidence of foreign influences. The Gate, although it has presented many plays by Irish authors and on Irish themes, is not a national theatre. It is simply a theatre. Its policy is the exploitation of all forms of theatrical expression regardless of nationality. It embraces upon occasion, the naturalistic play, but its concern has always been with the whole gamut of the stage.

The whole gamut of the stage, and all forms of theatrical expression really are represented in the Gate's long and distinguished list of productions. Indeed, this list might stand as a model for what a vital repertory theatre should do. The Gate presented examples of about everything from Aeschylus to Brecht — including fourteen of Shakespeare's plays, eleven of Shaw's including the complete *Back to Methuselah*, three of Ibsen, two of Chekhov, two of Strindberg, and six of Wilde including Mac Liammóir's adaptation of *Dorian Gray*, as well as traditional English classics by Congreve, Vanbrugh, Farquhar, and Sheridan. Yet despite this commitment to the classics, the larger part of the Gate's plays were drawn from what was the most theatrically exciting in the contemporary world drama. By 'theatrically exciting', I mean that the Gate's bent was toward the drama as theatre rather than, necessarily, as literature. Noël Coward, Guy Bolton, and Kaufman and Hart were produced nearly as often as Pirandello, Kaiser and Cocteau. Americans were well represented too, with seven plays by O'Neill, three by Rice, and others by Maxwell Anderson, Wilder, Behrman, Hellman, and Miller.

The Gate also produced a respectable number of new plays by Irishmen. Its most notable discovery was Denis Johnston, whose brilliant experimental early work is one of the theatre's major glories. It also produced a couple of plays by Yeats, Austin Clarke's *The Hunger Demon*, Richard Rowley's *Apollo in Mourne*, Padraic Pearse's *The Singer*, Padraic Colum's *Mogu of the Desert*, and St. John Ervine's

Shakespearian sequel *The Lady of Belmont*. There was realistic work like Frank Carney's *The Doctor's Boy*, the plays of Robert Collis, M. J. Farrell's *Guardian Angel*, Andrew Ganly's *Murder Like Charity*, Elsie Schauffler's *Parnell*. There were two plays by Lennox Robinson, two by Donagh MacDonagh, three by Mary Manning including the incomparable *Youth's the Season . . . ?*, three by Maura Laverty, four by David Sears. And in more recent years there has been the internationally acclaimed early work of Brian Friel such as *Philadelphia, Here I Come*, and even more recently the first and very interesting plays of Desmond Forristal. Even though the creation of an Irish dramatic literature was not the theatre's primary concern, this is an impressive list of new Irish work.

Nevertheless, if there is criticism to be levelled at the Gate, it is probably here, at its strongest point, its repertoire, that it should be levelled. My own biased feeling is that the great theatres of the world have primarily produced new plays, have nurtured and kept their dramatists, have created an individual voice, rather than brilliantly donned a hundred borrowed styles. But perhaps to ask such an earnest intensity in seeking out the most fervent of the best is simply to ask that the Gate have been something different. And would we have wanted that, wanted the Gate to have lost its insouciance, its frivolity, its delight in the gay, the frivolous, the silly, the witty? It had, of course, other and more sombre preoccupations than boulevard comedy, but, as one of its best productions suggests, the importance of being earnest implies also the necessity of being frivolous.

What, then, has the company given the nation? I should say expertise and craft, education and a honing of taste, a growth of urbane tolerance and a lessening of parochialism, a series of masterpieces that inspired terror, a series of nonsenses that evoked delight. In short, a civilised ideal. In short, Art.

Micheál Mac Liammóir in *Don Juan in Hell* by Bernard Shaw, 1973 revival. Photo : Fergus Bourke.

DR. MICHAEL SCOTT, FRIAI

architect of the Dublin Gate, the new Abbey Theatre, the Radio Telefís Eireann complex, among many important buildings. Michael Scott is also chairman of the Dublin Theatre Festival

The stage of the Gate theatre, drawn by J. W. Buchanan, 1935.

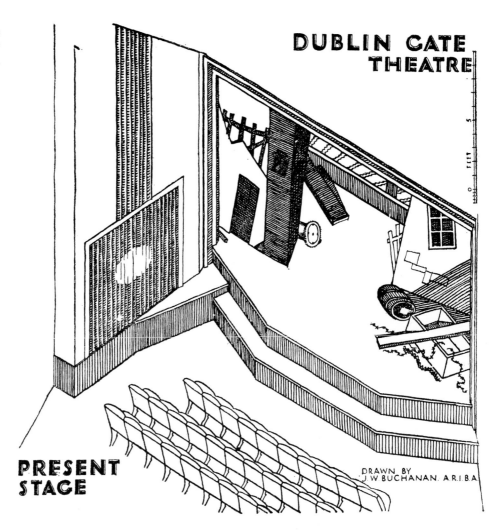

DUBLIN GATE THEATRE

PRESENT STAGE

DRAWN BY
J W BUCHANAN. A.R.I.B.A.

Perhaps I should begin by stating that I designed the Peacock Theatre when I was a pupil in the firm of Jones and Kelly. When I left this firm they let me take the job with me. The Peacock was situated in an old house between the Abbey Theatre and Abbey Street. It held 101 seats, the stage was tiny and there was no proscenium. On this stage Hilton Edwards achieved a remarkable production of *Peer Gynt* and played the principal part himself. This was followed by an equally remarkable production by Hilton of Denis Johnston's *The Old Lady Says No!* when Micheál Mac Liammóir played brilliantly the principal part. Indeed, I also played a small part in this production. After the experience of producing these plays under difficult conditions it was decided to find larger premises. Eventually the old concert hall in the Rotunda became available for conversion into what was to become the Gate Theatre. It was a large and splendid eighteenth-century room with a platform at the other end of the present stage. Hilton and myself worked feverishly on this project; we had very little money to solve all our problems. Hilton and I would go down to the Corporation and interview Mr. Higginbotham who was then in charge of buildings of public resort. These meetings were turbulent, to say the least, the Corporation wishing us to do all sorts of things for the protection of the public and the comfort of the players. However, just before we opened the Theatre, the Corporation insisted on us putting in steel tie-bars under the auditorium floor, which to this day, I still think was unnecessary. They appear in the ceiling of the lovely ballroom underneath and scar this architectural gem.

Also there were two toilets for men and women erected in the nine-teenth century and these we had to adapt with fittings and new flush doors. Micheál Mac Liammóir had these doors painted black with the words 'Fir' and 'Mna' in gold leaf, the only extravagance in the whole buildings. When Mr. Higginbotham came to pass the theatre for the Opening, he asked me what did these words mean and I said 'men and women'. Then he said they must be put on in English. He asked the foreman would he know which was which and the foreman said he would have to look in and see where the stand-up was. Micheál was so insensed at the Corporation's insistence on English that he instructed the painter to put the two words in eight languages underneath the English.

A disaster occurred on the opening night which was bitterly cold and the electrical heating system failed. Everybody was frozen stiff. A few days later, when we had the final cost of the reconstruction, it was found impossible to pay the bills and a meeting of creditors was held on the stage in the set of Dr. Faustus. We all took the sum of 5/- (five shillings) in settlement.

Eventually, thirty years after the opening night, Lord Longford was asked to do more reconstruction, such as putting in a concrete entrance stairs and other works for the safety and convenience of the public and players. Nine years ago when we found dry rot in the roof, we re-decorated the interior and made the stage more flexible by adding to the fore-stage and making an entrance on each side of the proscenium so the actors could reach this fore-stage free of the main stage. We also put the control for the stage lighting above at the back of the theatre where, of course, it should be.

That was forty-eight years ago. I have built a great many things since then, including theatres. But the memory of those days of making the Gate are precious. It was an experience never to be forgotten. Micheál and Hilton are, and always will be, unique in the history of theatre.

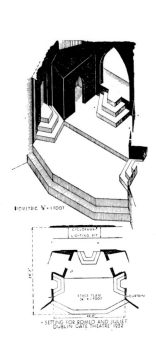

ISOMETRIC ¼" = 1 FOOT

SETTING FOR ROMEO AND JULIET
DUBLIN GATE THEATRE 1932

BRIAN FRIEL
author and playwright

To be invited to contribute to a testimonial to the achievements of Hilton Edwards and Micheál Mac Liammóir presents me with an opportunity and a problem. The opportunity is welcome: to be able to express publicly my great affection and great admiration for these two great men of the Irish theatre. The problem is one of style: to express that affection, admiration and gratitude without slipping into the accepted mode and language that this kind of occasion usually expresses itself in.

And my objection is not so much to the accepted form, excessive though it sometimes is, as to the notion it sometimes evokes — that we are all paying due tribute to lives completed, work done and finished with, accomplishments packed away and without reverberation (and I am writing this very shortly after Micheál's passing). Because that is not what we are doing. We are in fact celebrating two distinguished and vital presences whose work continues and whose continuing presence in the theatre in Ireland will be experienced for many decades to come.

My education with Hilton and Micheál began in 1963. Before that I had taken a few stumbling steps into drama. I then went to the United States where I learned what I could. In the years following my return to Ireland I wrote four plays, all of which Hilton directed and Micheál designed. Hilton was then in his early sixties, Micheál a few years older, with over three hundred productions under their belt. I was thirty-four, with two flawed plays behind me. And for the next five years we worked together in Ireland and in England and in America. I like to think that I came into their lives at a point when they were ready for something new. I know that they came into my life at a point when their practical skill and their vast experience and their scholarship were of most value to me. I am not aware that I have any theatrical pedigree; but if I had to produce documentation I would be pleased to claim — to paraphrase Turgenev's comment on Gogol — that I came out from under the Edwards-Mac Liammóir overcoat.

Fifty years of continuous work. In any country it would be a remarkable achievement. In a country the size of Ireland, with a theatrical tradition going back only to the turn of the century and with a population of less than four million people, the achievement is staggering. At some future date theatre historians will make their assessments of what that achievement precisely was and is and will be. But at this point I would offer two suggestions for consideration. (I wonder occasionally why is it that in all those years the Gate never produced a major writer as the Provincetown Players produced O'Neill, the Moscow Art Theatre Chekhov, the Abbey Synge and O'Casey. I have no answers. Perhaps it is simply that the concurrence of the power of the man and the power of the moment is totally fortuitous, and that the existence of a theatre and a company and a vibrant milieu are less important for a dramatist than we think.)

The first suggestion is this: that Hilton and Micheál endowed Irish theatre with stylishness. (Not a style. To talk about a 'Gate style' in the way we were once able to talk about an 'Abbey style' would be misleading. The manner in which plays are done at the Gate theatre is indeed distinctive in Ireland but by no means unique in these islands.) They offered us, insisted on, almost flaunted this stylishness during the years when the native drama saw 'truth' only in cloth caps and naturalistic speech and peasant quality. Stylishness was their essence. Everything they touched, from Anouilh to Zola, was graced by it. Stylishness was their truth, their authenticity, their epiphany. I think it has been more important to us than 'a style' because through it they rescued us from an indulgence in our most narrow and most provincial concept of ourselves. Nothing terrifies the stage-Irishman more than the mention of the word Gate.

The second suggestion — and perhaps it derives from the first — is that Hilton and Micheál insisted on a firm and final distinction between the professional and the amateur theatre. Never in their theatre were the borders blurred. When Hilton wrote ten years ago in *The Mantle of Harlequin*, 'I am not helped by an ignoble but irradicable tradition of professionalism that inclines me to shirk a too close contact with amateur activities', he was not expressing an erratic fastidiousness. He was distinguishing, as an artist must, between affection and passion, between flirtation and commitment, between interest and belief, between a habit and a life. To people who are not Irish it must seem strange that these distinctions have to be expressed and insisted on. But Hilton, wise in his English blood, knows the necessity. And his and Micheál's total dedication to a life in the theatre, a life pursued persistently, joyously, flamboyantly, almost in ignorance that any other was available, has made the professional theatre a possibility for all of us. From 1928 on the way was demonstrably there.

Hilton and Micheál, friends and mentors, I salute you both.

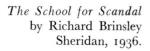

The School for Scandal by Richard Brinsley Sheridan, 1936.

JOHN FINEGAN

drama critic

One of the regrets of my life as a theatregoer is that I never saw the miracles performed over several months in 1928 and 1929 by Hilton Edwards and Micheál Mac Liammóir on the tiny stage of the original Peacock Theatre.

Finance, not disinterest or ignorance, was the cause. Seats at the Peacock, with accommodation for only 102 patrons, cost three-and-sixpence, a sum substantial enough then to put a drain on my pocket money. At the Abbey at that time a seat could be had for a shilling.

So it was at the Gate, to which the Edwards-MacLiammóir Company had moved in February 1930 after two seasons at the Peacock, that I had my first sighting of two men who were to have a considerable effect on my life, first as paying theatregoer, later as a writer on the theatre. Seats in the last three or four rows at the Gate were, I gladly discovered, no more than a shilling each, and so came within my budget.

My first visit to what I was later to call the glittering Gate was during the initial season there. It was a double bill that evening in early May, 1930: *Simoom* by Strindberg as curtain-raiser, followed by an affectionate send-up of William Pratt's Victorian melodrama, *Ten Nights in a Bar-Room.*

I was fascinated by the harrowing drama of *Simoom*, which had Coralie Carmichael as an Arab girl practising mental torture on an officer of the Zouaves, played by Micheál Mac Liammóir, then in his early manhood and looking like a god. Hilton Edwards, cast as the girl's lover, was the third player.

The Pratt melodrama, with those three players, reinforced by Meriel Moore, Madame Kirkwood Hackett, Michael Scott and Mitchel Cogley, among others, was infused with a romping, infectious gaiety of a kind I had never before experienced on the stage. I walked home to Dolphin's Barn, my head in the air, clutching the orange-covered programme, which is one of my prized possessions.

Thereafter during the nineteen-thirties I was a frequent visitor at the Gate. It was a decade of Edwards-Mac Liammóir presentations unmatched in scope and brilliance.

Picking at random, there were Jenssen's hypnotic drama, *The Witch*; the Gate's first Shakespeare, *The Merchant of Venice*, with Hilton a dignified Shylock, all cringing obliterated, and with Micheál a radiantly-romantic Bassanio to Meriel Moore's graceful Portia; the first Christmas revue, *Christmas Pie*; the sweep and beauty of *Tzar Paul*; the style and elegance of *Lady Windermere's Fan*, the Gate's first presentation of a play by Oscar Wilde, to be followed by *An Ideal Husband* and *The Importance of Being Earnest*, with Cyril Cusack and Micheál as Wilde's men about town; the disturbing romanticism of *Death Takes a Holiday*; the vampire terrors of le Fanu's *Carmilla*; *Marrowbone Lane, Lady Precious Stream, A Midsummer Night's Dream.*

I remember *Jew Suss*, a famous first night, with Hilton taut and compelling in the title role, Betty Chancellor ethereal as Naomi, and the 16-year-old, dynamic new arrival, Orson Welles, astonishingly confident as a lecherous eighteenth-century German duke; there was Mary Manning's witty Dublin comedy, *Youth's the Season—?*, of which I recall most vividly Micheál's adroit performance while perched on a ladder supposedly painting or wall-papering; I remember *Romeo and Juliet*, with Micheál and Meriel heart-stopping as the young lovers; and a revival of a 1929 Civic Week pagent, *The Ford of the Hurdles*, by Micheál, whose delivery of Emmet's speech from the dock reverberates sharp and clear in the memory.

But the achievements of the 1930s in which Hilton, as he did earlier in the Peacock, conquered space decades long before the Americans and the Russians, were almost endless — Molnar's *Liliom*, with one of Micheál's favourite roles, that of a fairground worker; the sexually-oppressive *Children in Uniform*; *Wuthering Heights*, with Micheál a passionate Heathcliffe and Ria Mooney a piercing Catherine; *Blood and Sand*, blistering as a Mediterranean noonday; *Crime and Punishment*, with, for the Gate, an incredible quadrupled setting; *Macbeth*, with Hilton as the Thane, unforgettable in the 'Tomorrow and Tomorrow' speech; *Victoria Regina*; Denis Johnston's exciting and puzzling *Bride for the Unicorn*; a revival of *Peer Gynt* that held us in our seats long after the chimes at midnight; *Richard of Bordeaux*; *A School for Scandal*; *Berkeley Square*; *Mourning Becomes Electra*; Hilton as Richard III, as Swift, as Cyrano de Bergerac; I could go on for pages.

I must mention a knife-edged *Julius Caesar*, with the 25-year-old James Mason a powerfully-articulate Brutus and with Micheál as Mark Antony sending shivers down the spine with his impassioned delivery of 'Cry havoc, and let slip the dogs of war!' There was an uplifting and expansive production of Ibsen's *Brand* — one of Hilton's greatest triumphs as a director — with Micheál haunting as the disaster-prone preacher (a presentation on which the partners lost a considerable amount of money because of unexpectedly poor support).

Above all, I revelled in the revivals of *The Old Lady Says No!*, which had been the Company's last production in the Peacock in 1929. Denis Johnston's searing satire has the most arresting opening to any Irish drama that I know. While the curtain is still down there is heard the approaching tramp of marching feet, and voices chant the 'Sean Bhean Bhocht'. The tramping and the singing continue for some minutes before gradually dying away. The curtain then rises.

The play, as directed, indeed orchestrated, by Hilton Edwards, has never ceased to move me; neither have its original performers — Hilton as Major Sirr, Meriel Moore's double portrayal of contrasted Irelands, and Micheál's Speaker (Robert Emmet), with red lightning tightening in his blood as he wanders, bewildered, through an unthinking twentieth-century Dublin — been equalled.

Micheál's first *Hamlet* in the early 1930's I was unable to see — I couldn't get a seat. I had to wait ten years before experiencing his study of the Prince, in a modern dress production ('Hamlet in a lounge suit', said a heading).

In the early 1930's we read in the newspapers how Lord Longford, when financial crisis struck the Gate, came to the rescue, symbolically waving his cheque book at a meeting of shareholders. Four years later, in the mid 1930's, while Hilton and Micheál were on a tour of Egypt, we learned that Lord Longford had formed a company of his own at the Gate. For weeks we had no clear idea that an unfortunate split had occurred, and the full, sad story was not revealed until Micheál published the first volume of his reminiscences, *All For Hecuba*, a seminal book of the Irish theatre. The eventual healing, in the 1950's, of the breach gave satisfaction to every lover of the Gate.

In the Spring of 1940 the Edwards-Mac Liammóir Company paid its first visit to the Gaiety Theatre, opening with the premiere of Micheál's fantasy, *Where Stars Walk*. At the Gate patrons were attuned to surprises. When, at the Gaiety, the curtain rose to reveal a stage in total darkness and a voice speaking in Irish we nudged one another and whispered, 'The Gate hasn't changed.' It was one of Micheál's wittiest touches. After a few minutes the stage lights came on, the English tongue was heard, and the confirmed Gaiety patrons were able to breathe comfortably again.

Then, also at the Gaiety, came *Antony and Cleopatra*, with towering sets never since equalled on the Dublin stage, and towering performances from Micheál and Meriel in the title roles. Also in the same theatre there were *Blithe Spirit, The Man Who Came to Dinner, Rebecca, Othello*, a new carnival-style *Merchant of Venice*; Micheál's enchanting *I'll Met By Moonlight*, and *Ghosts*, with nerve-tingling portrayals by Sybil Thorndike as the mother and Micheál as her afflicted son.

In the 1950's came *Liffey Lane* and *Tolka Row*, with Micheál playing an old man for the first time in his career; *Death of a Salesman*; *Saint Joan*; *Ring Round the Moon*; *The Lark*; *Oedipus Rex* and *Mother Courage*.

Micheál's splendid adaptation of the Liam O'Flaherty novel, *The Informer*, was staged at the Olympia to considerable acclaim, with the adaptor eloquent and powerful in the title role.

An elaborate and richly-beautiful presentation of Pirandello's *Henry IV*, with Micheál as the mad king, threw the Company into severe financial difficulties, because of the expense involved and lack of support. The difficulties were to some extent alleviated (those were the years before a subsidy of any kind) by Micheál appearing with Jimmy O'Dea in Gaiety pantomimes and revues.

And so on to a first night of tingling excitement, a night that is lodged forever in the memory of all who were present in the Gaiety on 23 September 1960 — the premiere, during the Theatre Festival, of *The Importance of Being Oscar*. Micheál's solo evocation of Wilde, his characters and his period, was spell-binding.

Enthusiastically, I wrote in *The Evening Herald* that this assuredly was an entertainment for the stages of the world. I was happy to find my prediction coming true within a few years.

I first met Micheál backstage at the Gate in December 1943. A few weeks earlier I had begun writing a weekly theatre column in *The Evening Herald*, and I had gone round after a performance of *Wuthering Heights* to enquire the number of plays he had written up to that time. He scribbed the titles on a slip of paper and said, 'Why not come to tea some afternoon, and we can discuss the plays more fully?'

A couple of days later I presented myself at No. 4 Harcourt Terrace, a Regency house I was to know well in the years that followed. In the spacious, first-floor, book-lined drawing-room, with its paintings by Norah McGuinness, Louis le Brocquy and Mac Liammóir himself, I was introduced to Hilton, who was discussing with his partner the forthcoming Christmas presentation of the revue, *Punchbowl*.

It was the first of many memorable visits to No. 4, where I learned more about the practical side of theatre and the art of the actor than I could ever learn from books. Hilton and Micheál were the most encouraging of mentors.

Of the fascinating *All For Hecuba*, Micheál's first autobiography, I have a particularly vivid memory. On a Saturday forenoon early in 1946 Micheál phoned saying he would like to see me urgently at lunchtime. Could I call round?

In the drawing-room at No. 4 he showed me a proof copy of his book and told me it needed an index, but that someone to whom he had entrusted the task had made little or no progress. Could I do an index? I told him I had never indexed a book before, but I'd try, and asked, 'When is it wanted?'

'I'm afraid I have to get it away to the publishers by Monday afternoon,' Micheál said. Because of editorial duty until midnight that Saturday I wasn't able to start on the index until early on Sunday morning. I had the advantage of knowing many of the people mentioned in the pages. By 8 a.m. on Monday, after almost twenty-four hours' work I had completed and checked the index and handed it to Micheál in time for the post. I was very happy to be associated in this small way with a treasured book.

In the early summer of 1947 Micheál was in Paris, staying in the small hotel in the Rue Stanislas owned by the family Jeanne. Hilton was, I think, touring with Orson Welles somewhere in Europe. Micheál invited me to stay at the hotel on my way back from a Swiss holiday.

Liliom, one of Micheál's best-liked plays, in which he had appeared many times at the Gate, was that summer running at a theatre in Montparnasse. One evening we went along to see it. At the box office Micheál took out his wallet to pay for seats when the manager, who was standing nearby, recognised him, brushed aside the notes, and invited both of us to be his guests in the principal box.

On another night Micheál expressed a wish to see the revue at the Casino de Paris in Montmartre. We managed to get a taxi to the theatre and saw the spectacular show. At 1 a.m., after a drink or two in the Place Pigalle, there wasn't a taxi to be had and the last Metro train had gone. We had a few more drinks to fortify ourselves and then began a five-mile walk across Paris. Footsore, we reached the Rue Stanislas as dawn was breaking over the city.

At Dublin rehearsals which I sometimes attended in the early years of the *Herald* column I had occasionally observed actors, on the first or second rung of the ladder, become argumentative with the particular director. Micheál was Hilton's partner, but never at a Gate rehearsal did I see him question Hilton's authority and, at times, his criticism. It was the measure of Micheál's loyalty to his profession.

I am honoured to have had the friendship of those two men of genius, and to have seen most of their finest productions — Hilton Edwards, the most brilliant director in our theatre and, as I once wrote, the most popular Englishman who ever came to live among us; Micheál Mac Liammóir, the greatest Irish actor of this century.

TERENCE DE VERE WHITE

novelist, short-story writer, member of the board of directors of the
Dublin Gate Theatre, and former literary editor of *The Irish Times*

Queuing up for seats in the gallery or upper circle or pit was so much
a part of the routine of going to the theatre in Dublin when I was young
that it counted as part of the entertainment. I saw Micheál and
Hilton for the first time after a wait of two hours at the box office for
the McMaster and Doran seasons at the Abbey and Gaiety theatres
respectively.

Hilton came first. He was playing small parts for even smaller money;
and I must confess that I have acquired this knowledge from playbills
he has shown me. As these include an actor called Ralph Richardson,
and I can't remember him from Adam, I needn't apologise to Hilton
Edwards. It is a curious reflection that one only remembers Doran, who
was so woefully bad, and in that respect outstanding; and, of course,
he hogged all the good parts in true actor-manager tradition. In those
days, when enthusiasm overflowed and the critical sense was in the bud,
total absorption in what was happening on stage stifled discrimination;
but even then I knew that Doran was inadequate. He looked wrong; he
sounded wrong; he was wrong. By a sort of alchemy he made all
Shakespeare's heroes into one — Charles Doran. He should have played
parish priests, village worthies, inn keepers, customs officials; but he
followed the example of Benson (an incomparably more talented performer) who led a team of juveniles more gifted than himself and sub-
ordinated them to his dominion. They learnt from Benson; Doran had
nothing to teach, and no one of any account stayed with him for long;
not Hilton, certainly. Doran provided very little bread and no butter
when these were in short supply for all but a fortunate few at the
beginning of their acting careers. Travelling companies solved the
pressing problem of survival while waiting to be recognised. I was — and
am still — grateful to Doran for having given me the first opportunity
to see Shakespeare.

Doran came before McMaster; and after that portly, priestly presence,
the younger man shone like Lucifer. He had considerable manly beauty,
a true actor's voice and carriage. All sufficient for a young actor; if
there was a lack of cerebration, it didn't matter then. With Esmé Biddle,
who was what used to be called 'a fine-looking woman', he added a new
excitement to life. Gladly I queued for him.

It was in one of McMaster's productions of *Macbeth* at the Abbey
that I saw Micheál for the first time. I can see him quite clearly in my
mind's eye, delivering a speech rather hurriedly, but only a dumb ox
could fail to notice an actor out of the ordinary. In the matter of height,
he was at a disadvantage with his brother-in-law (I didn't know they
were brothers-in-law or anything about Micheál then and if I noticed
a lack of inches it was because I must have scented a rival to the reigning
champion and notched up all the points in his favour. Youth is loyal;
and I was jealous for him).

Mac Liammóir had already made his impression when I heard his praises being sung in Galway by Liam O'Brian, who had the Chair of French in U.C.G. That must have been in the Autumn of 1928. The occasion was an inter-university debate. I was one of the representatives of Trinity College's Historical Society, and at sixteen the youngest. When the visitors went for a walk with the Professor, and he rhapsodised about the wonders Mac Liammóir had done for the Gaelic theatre in Galway, I wished to myself that he had established another sort of theatre (and nearer home) if he was half the marvel the Professor said he was. I must have brashly said something to this effect because I have a recollection of a shadow passing over the geniality of the monologue, and now I am ashamed, because such an Irish theatre was the only way at the time to counteract with genius and good manners the unimaginative strategy of the Department of Education down the years.

However, the Gods were listening to me. As we were talking the Gate in Dublin was about to open. It brought world theatre to Dublin and as well a higher standard of theatrical professionalism than Dublin had probably ever known. And not merely on a visit, it was to stay as part of our daily life. Soon it became world known, attracting the marvellous boy, Orson Welles, and a lower-keyed James Mason, recently down from Cambridge, knocking at the door in the West End.

The nucleus of what was then, to all intents, a permanent company included, with the two partners, Betty Chancellor and Meriel Moore, a quartet that in a wide variety of plays could hold their own in any company. I heard Golding Bright, then the most influential dramatic agent in London, say when Betty left the stage after her success in *Spring Meeting* that she was the most promising comedienne of her generation.

Until the Gate was established there was no opportunity to see international theatre in Dublin. Lady Gregory had Kiltartanised Molière for the Abbey. I have read but never saw the result on the stage. Nobody has ever asked for its disinterment. The Gate company was equipped to put on such plays without their being first processed for local consumption. This is not said in disparagement of the Abbey; it had established its own tradition, racy of the soil; but if there was to be a truly national theatre, it should have been capable of performing convincingly Goldsmith, Sheridan, Wilde, Shaw — and if we stretch a point to claim them — Congreve and Farquhar. Beckett was still to come. When the Abbey was burnt down in 1951, a god-sent opportunity was missed to join forces and establish such a theatre. It would have been a living and perpetual memorial to Irish genius. Ria Mooney, then working in the Abbey, would have been a useful ally in any bridge-building. Instead, under the genial dictatorship of a man with no training in the theatre, the Abbey was cramped in the performance of a dual purpose, the production of plays and the guarding of the language. Remembering Galway, Mac Liammóir could have lent a golden touch to the Blythe spirit. And what is class-consciously called 'the Anglo-Irish tradition' would have become common stock.

Of recent years the Abbey has not been shy about putting on the plays in which the Gate excelled; but the Gate has never attempted to play in the Abbey's garden. Once, it took in an Abbey reject. Denis Johnston's *The Old Lady Says No!*, backed by fifty of the Abbey's green pounds, was a resounding success at the Gate; and this play might be invoked to demonstrate the psychic difference between these theatres.

The *Old Lady* had all the appearance of having been hand-made for the Gate, and nobody who has seen Micheál's Robert Emmet — his best part? — will ever be satisfied with any other.

What was the Hilton-Micheál secret? It is not sufficient to say that two highly talented and professionally instructed men of the theatre happened to set up shop in Dublin. This is not a case of two and two making four. The addition of these talents made resoundingly five. Such partnerships are rare, and in recent history I can think of only one other, Somerville and Ross. Usually they are short-lived; an irreconcilable clash of personalities breaks them up, as, unhappily, Gilbert and Sullivan. Or they are not true mergers. There was never really any such animal as the Chester-Belloc, for instance.

Yeats and Lady Gregory worked close together as, at the same period, did Shaw and Granville-Barker; but the Edwards-Mac Liammóir combination is unique. The extent each has helped the other is known only to themselves. How two personalities so strong and individual could have kept in step during that fifty-year march is a mystery, perhaps a miracle. Master of lighting and stage direction that he is, Hilton — as anyone who saw *Equus* in London and Dublin can testify — can give to any play that works on the stage an added dimension and a Turner glow. Enough to be thankful for if he weren't such an accomplished actor. The younger generation hardly realises of what it has been deprived by his diffidence unless they saw his Herod in Conor Cruise O'Brien's play, a monologue that required a virtuoso to hold the attention of an audience. I venture to say no actor in this country could have answered so overwhelmingly all the demands of that part or made the argument seem so vital. That triumph recalled his earliest, and some who saw it still maintain, his finest — *Peer Gynt*. If the Gate had to be remembered by one production only, my vote would be for that.

I am sorry the partners have not played Ibsen more often. Some of Mac Liammóir's best performances were in Ibsen roles under other managements. His Brack to Dame Peggy Ashcroft's Hedda Gabler in London was first rate. One of the most inspired performances I have ever seen was Sybil Thorndike's Mrs. Alving in *Ghosts*. So far from being put in shadow by that white-hot blaze, Micheál surpassed himself as the despairing Oswald. Sybil Thorndike's marvellous acting brought out a 'something extra' that in the ordinary course was not demanded of him. For the same reason I believe he showed his acting ability better in parts which have refused to adapt themselves to the demands of his personality. Where he had to get behind another mask and animate it, he — or so its seemed to me — gave the actor in him fuller scope. Even Hamlet was not allowed to be merely Prince of Denmark; as the Mac Liammóir hat fitted, he had perforce to wear it, as had many other less noble than he. I believe Micheál gave his best performances in unlikely parts — in Emlyn Williams's *Night Must Fall* and as Gyppo Nolan in O'Flaherty's *The Informer*, for instance.

He came truly into his own with *The Importance of Being Oscar*, which became part of theatrical history in his lifetime. Here was the perfect vehicle for his talents. Wilde, so utterly sympathetic to him, was a mould into which he could pour his own personality, a mirror in which he saw his own reflection. At sixty Micheál came into his kingdom. It was worth waiting for.

All too easy to say he should always have done one-man shows. After

Micheál Mac Liammóir as Robert Emmet in *The Old Lady Says No!*

Wilde there were suggestions in plenty for other candidates. Yeats was most generously put together for a charity matinée, and was often performed with satisfactory results, but it lacked the empathy of the Wilde, being not so much a portrait of the poet as a tribute to the inspiration he gave to the actor's formative years. In the later poetry, the public man, the spook-chaser, the literary lion, Mac Liammóir took no interest. It had nothing to do with the world of his own imagination. Therefore he put more heart into *I must be Talking to My Friends* and contemplated a new theatrical form — a stage autobiography. Art must be life at one remove, and we need not regret that this project never left the drawing-board. Boswell put his best into his Doctor Johnson; Micheál gave us Oscar Wilde. It was an inimitable medley of understanding, wit, humour, sympathy, mimicry, vocal beauty and artistic tact. I wish I could have seen Hilton as Volpone and Micheál as Malvolio. But that must be added to the long list of the theatre's might-have-beens. And there is so much else to thank them for.

For a start, an ego-trip. I claim to be the only man in history to have interpolated my own spontaneous Shakespearen gloss into a Hilton Edwards production of *Macbeth*.

It happened in the old Cork Opera House, a charming and homely Victorian relic which had the unusual amenity of a back-stage bar — though that amenity has no direct bearing on my story. The time was the autumn of 1938: the Gate company was playing a fortnight's repertory at the Opera House, and I had the good fortune to be introduced to Hilton, Micheál, and the rest of them by Seán and Geraldine Neeson. Back in 1927 when the two young actors were touring with Anew McMaster and Hilton caught pneumonia in Cobh, the Neesons took them in during Hilton's convalescence. They arranged a concert recital for Hilton, who had a fine baritone voice, and an exhibition of his own drawings and paintings for Micheál, and I have always understood that it was in the Neeson's hospitable house, Mount Verdon Villa, that the boys first discussed the possibility of founding their own little theatre. Certainly to this day there hangs on a wall of Geraldine Neeson's drawing-room Micheál's first draft of the original Gate's programme cover design — Harlequin drawing aside the proscenium curtains.

To revert to my Shakespearean amendment: because I had red hair and a bony angular frame, Hilton had chosen me from a mob of amateur walkers-on to play the part of the leading Scottish vassal. We carried banners and pikes and bushes from Birnam Wood to Dunsinane, and our big moment came in the banqueting scene when I led my troop along a ramp bearing trays with goblets and platters, and then set the table for the Court and Banquo's ghost. Hilton was Macbeth, Coralie Carmichael was Lady Mac, and the young Christopher Casson was sweating over MacDuff's lines. The interior setting, very Scottish-Gothic, was by Molly McEwen, and I can still hear the eerie theme-music chosen by Hilton for the fog-bound tragedy of the Thane and his lady.

My costume was an abbreviated kilt, and the sandals that went with it were about half an inch longer than my feet. The Vassals, with their vessels, made their way on to the ramp from the wings by using a prop-hamper as a step.

The scene is set. On the first night all was excitement, and the blood-boltered play held a packed Opera House spellbound. Observing strict —well, almost total—discipline, I drank only one half-pint of Murphy's in the stage bar at the beginning of the show, and when the cue came for the big entrance to the banqueting hall I felt like John Barrymore. Off we started, me at the head of my team with a laden tray in my two hands. What I didn't know was that Cecil Monson, the stage manager of the time, had left the essential prop-hamper with the lid unlocked and the open end of it towards me. So — as I stepped on to it, my projecting sandal caught on the projecting lip; the lid of the hamper came up with my leg, and Number One Vassal, with tray and goblets, fell on to the stage, with goblets rolling in every direction. I forgot all about the Barrymore bit, lifted myself on one elbow, and uttered a short, sharp, sibilant monosyllable that even Shakespeare never used at his bawdiest. It brought the house down, particularly the Gods — and from that day to this Hilton never said one word about it. I need hardly say that I never mentioned it to him, either.

That was a superb tour. The other Shakespearean production was *Hamlet*, with Hilton as Claudius, Coralie as Gertrude, Meriel Moore as Ophelia, and the most memorable Hamlet Ireland has seen in this century from Micheál, then in his artistic prime. It was on that tour, too, that I experienced the first paralysing impact of *The Old Lady* . . . Hilton has described Denis Johnston's dramatic *tour-de-force* as 'a concerto with the Speaker as soloist', and it is arguable that Micheál, as the Speaker, gave the finest performance in a lifetime of fine performances. Inevitably, when Sirr's soldiery stunned and concussed the Speaker in the first five minutes of the play and an agitated stage-manager appealed for a doctor, a sober-suited specialist from Patrick's Hill left his stalls seat and rushed round backstage — but then that, I'm told, happened on every first night of the play, everywhere. At the end of that first Cork production of *The Old Lady* . . . , the entire audience was drunk with the bitter magic of the play. Hilton's masterly direction and lighting, and the symphonic playing of the company.

I'm not sure if it was then or in another Cork season that Hilton hypnotised the *bourgeoisie* of West Cork and their families with his great bawdy characterisation as Sir John Brute in *The Provok'd Wife*. In any case I recall that there were some rollicking post-show parties — at Neeson's—with Hilton singing a resonant 'Lord Randal'. On another occasion somewhere up the Lee, Micheál demonstrated one of his myriad gifts by reproducing in perfect tempo on the piano a Scarlatti sonatina which he'd just heard for the first time — but transposed to the key of C — the only key in which he could play.

When I saw them first they were well established in the Gate, and the first show I saw was *Death Takes a Holiday* in 1937, but I'd have given a lot to be around in their heady early days at the Peacock, with *Peer Gynt*, and again *The Old Lady*. . . . Only the indomitable and resourceful Hilton Edwards could have survived the production problems imposed by the Peacock's physical limitations, but he did, and from the first night of *Peer Gynt* the company played to full houses, with all the 102 seats filled.

Meanwhile, as Micheál tells so vividly in *All For Hecuba*, they had their inspirational vision of the building that was to become the Gate from a window in Groome's Hotel, and in December 1929 the lease for the annexe to the Rotunda was signed. On 17 February 1930, *Faust* opened there to an audience deep-frozen by a failed heating-plant. This and bad weather combined to keep audiences perilously sparse for the early productions in the new house, even though they offered one of Hilton's finest performances as Old Chris in *Anna Christie*, with Coralie Carmichael and Fred Johnston, but the rollicking and still remembered *Ten Nights in a Bar Room* later that Spring was a big popular success. Financially, however, the company was still tottering on the edge of disaster, and its survival was very doubtful until December 1930, when Lord Longford offered to play the angel, and though corporeally far from a cherub, continued in his angelic role for many years to come.

Indeed Edward, 6th Earl of Longford, continued to be the saviour of the Gate in a very real sense for many years after a clash of temperament on the Board of the original company caused him to found his own Longford Players in 1936. When the Dublin Corporation condemned the Gate building, he said that if the Gate fell down he would be standing among the ruins. It didn't come to that, but Edward Longford had the condemned theatre rebuilt, largely at his own expense, and for years afterwards could be seen in the streets of Dublin and in the foyer of the Gate collecting for the Gate Repair Fund. He also wrote a number of plays, the most notable of them *Yahoo* — the best play on Swift, and *Carmilla*, as well as doing some notable translations of Greek tragedies. His wife, Christine, too, contributed a number of plays to the theatre's repertory.

In many ways, the 1936 palace revolution in the original Gate was of great benefit to the Irish theatre. An arrangement whereby each company had tenancy of the mother house for six months of the year brought the Gate and Longford companies on provincial tours during the period they were 'out', and did a great deal, as did Anew McMaster, to widen the dramatic horizons of provincial theatregoers, thus laying the foundations of the flourishing amateur dramatic movement of today.

I never saw Micheál's Romeo, but I still remember his Richard II as vividly as I remember Hilton's malignant Iago and McMaster's sonorous Othello. There was a luscious *Anthony and Cleopatra*, too, at the Gaiety during the war, and it was during the first of those Gaiety seasons that we saw the best of Micheál's eleven plays. *Where Stars Walk* was infused with a sort of enchanted mystique in Mac Liammóir's interpretation of the Celtic god turned houseboy and in Merial Moore's maidservant-goddess. Yet the other side of this coin gave us drawing-room comedy as witty and brittle as Coward, but with an inimitable Dublin flavour. I still laugh when I remember the immortal Maureen Delaney at the Ouija-board, and the complete puzzlement of the visiting Englishman when Shelah Richards, as McCann, the battle-axe Dublin journalist, said 'How're ya' since?'

The Gaiety, too, saw the first production of another fine Mac Liammóir play, *Ill Met By Moonlight*, with Eithne Dunne superlatively good as Catherine, the changeling girl. It was there that Hilton exploited Siobhán McKenna's talents as a comedienne in *The Love of Four Colonels*, just as later he gave her the first production of *Saint Joan*, with Mac Liammóir, Jack McGowran and himself in support.

Siobhán's name reminds me of an aspect of the Gate that isn't always remembered — it was the training-stable for many stars. Twenty-four years ago Orson Welles was the lionised guest at a party given by John Huston in Elstree. He got together with me early on, and for about two hours talked with enormous affection, respect, and humour about his teen-age apprenticeship at the Gate with Hilton and Micheál. James Mason worked there, too, and from our own side of the Irish Sea the Gate gave some early opportunities to Geraldine Fitzgerald, Siobhán McKenna, Cyril Cusack and Jack McGowran, as well as Donal Donnelly, Paddy Bedford, and Milo O'Shea.

Welles remembered his old masters when he came to film *Othello*.

He cast Micheál as Iago and Hilton as Brabantio, and the experience resulted in one of the funniest books on film-making and Welles' kaleidoscopic court ever written — Mac Liammóir's *Put Money in Thy Purse*. The production of the film had its financial ups-and-downs, and Welles had problems in getting distribution and in paying his artists. Some years afterwards he made a part payment to Hilton and Micheál by taking on the part of the Narrator in Hilton's filmed ghost-story, *Return to Glenascaul*. The movie opened with Welles driving in the Dublin mountains on a very wet night. He came across a stalled car, its driver poking under the bonnet. Welles rolled down his window and asked 'Something wrong?'

'I'm having trouble with my distributor,' said the afflicted driver.

'So am I,' said Orson, and drove off in the rain. The private family joke remained in the film on its release.

When Micheál made his great come-back after the lean years, with *Oscar* in 1960, I went backstage to congratulate him at the end of the second week of the initial Gaiety run. He thanked me, and then said confidentially: 'I'm bored with it already, and I'm afraid I'll be stuck with it for the rest of my life.' He was, too, and towards the end I think he preferred his own marvellous tribute to the Ireland for whom and to whom he gave so much, *I Must be Talking to My Friends*.

His friends at last acknowledged Micheál and his partner by making them Freemen of the City of Dublin, and by conferring on both partners Honorary Doctorates. More practical acknowledgement was made by the State's subsidy to the Gate, but perhaps the finest expression of a nation's gratitude was made, in a way that is typically Irish, when what seemed to be the whole Irish nation, headed by the President and an ex-President of the Republic, turned out in love and homage as Micheál's coffin was borne from Newman's University church in March, 1978.

For fifty years the Mac Liammóir-Edwards partnership had lit the floor of magic for a public that at times must have seemed maddeningly indifferent to the pearls that were laid before it. At the end of that half century of indefatigable labour the treasures that had been lavished gained some part of the appreciation they so richly merited.

34

Micheál Mac Liammóir as *Hamlet*
at Kronberg Castle, 1952.

MARY MANNING
playwright, author and critic

Forty-seven years ago I first met Hilton Edwards and Micheál Mac Liammóir. At first the friendship was not beautiful. I was then working as a very junior drama critic on *The Irish Independent* and I gave one of their early Gate productions, I think it was *The Witch*, a rather brash review mentioning amongst other things the presence of 'two drunken seagulls'. Then as now where critics are concerned, Hilton was unpredictable. The reactions to my review were thunderous. I was invited to a director's meeting for some form of interrogation. During the proceedings I was indeed threatened with physical punishment by Hilton. I remember the others were kinder; the others being Edward Longford, Micheál, and Norman Reddin. I was so frightened I tottered down to Bewleys in Westmoreland Street, accompanied by a crazy but highly intelligent cousin of mine Jack Longford (no relation to Edward), and there I sobbed over my coffee and buns. I did no more reviewing; it was too frightening, but I did throw all my energies into writing a play. I was working in a lending library run by an alcoholic lady during the day time, so I had to work on my play at night. Jack Longford was in Trinity where he met Sam Beckett who was teaching there. Occasionally they both dropped in of an evening and drank cooking sherry in front of the fire and gave me advice about the play. Both advisors being of a naturally gloomy disposition they suggested the title *Youth's the Season*, with a large question mark. The question mark was of vital importance. Sam gave me the idea for Egosmith, the bartender, who never uttered a word throughout the play but listened to everyone. They both made me dare all things and send it to the Gate Theatre which very timidly and unhopefully I did. Imagine my surprise when I received a note from the Gate inviting me to come in and discuss the play in which they were definitely interested. I simply couldn't believe it when I arrived. Hilton was all affability, Micheál making jokes and calling me darling and Edward Longford beaming. Yes, they liked *Youth's the Season — ?* and they were definitely going to put it on. This time I laughed all the way to Bewleys and dear Jack was waiting for me there full of wild surmise and we celebrated over coffee and baked beans on toast. Alas Youth was the season for all of us then, and how brief a season it is, and now I would not add a question mark. None of my three plays performed at the Gate were ever revived; they were too much part of their period. Spring days, not good in winter!

My real job in the Gate and the one which meant most to me was the editorship of the Gate magazine *Motley*. The contributors were in the purest sense contributors for we could not afford to pay them. *Motley* was a monthly periodical, sometimes two months merged and it ceased operations during the summer months. My assistant was a forlorn character called Barbara Astley who also ran the Children's theatre. Getting the advertisements which were to be our financial mainstay was

The front cover
of *Motley* by
Micheál Mac Liammóir.

MOTLEY

36

a grim undertaking. Thumbing pensively through old copies I see Jammet's restaurant and the Victor Waddington galleries were our most loyal customers and oh, what triumph, twice we obtained two whole back pages advertising the Hospital Sweeps. Very often, alas, there were blank pages where there should have been advertisements, with a touching little paragraph high up in the right-hand corner begging our readers to realise that by supporting our advertisers they were supporting Irish industries. Because they were unpaid, and who'd blame them, the contributors were often late with their copy; the editing was rather haphazard and the spelling interestingly unconventional. Sometimes there were no letters received for the Correspondence Column and I had to write fake letters to myself signed by imaginary personalities. One character, Brenda Love, writing from her boarding school (for the daughters of gentlemen), frequently appeared in our pages. She was, it seemed, deeply infatuated with Micheál Mac Liammóir. 'I could not sleep at night wandering all about him' she wrote. Wandering, of course, was an unfortunate printer's error.

Amongst the many news items received one evoked considerable comment, some of it irreverent. 'The Elizabethan Dramatic Society (TCD) have asked me to state that they have decided to include men in the case of their June production and that they hope for very good results from this innovation!'

Considering our poverty, it was astonishing looking over the list after forty years, how many distinguished writers gave their talents to *Motley*. They included Frank O'Connor, Seán O'Faolain, Austin Clarke, Pádraic Colum, Francis Stuart, Richard Llewellyn Davis, John Betjeman, Blanaid Salkeld, Niall Montgomery, Niall Sheridan, and, of course, the directors of the Gate wrote copiously and often about themselves, their work, their hopes, and dreams, and sometimes their nightmares.

P. S. O'Hegarty contributed several scolding articles rather in the manner of a cross but fond Nanny who knew what was good for you. One called 'A Cold Bath for the Gate' immediately evoked a hot bath from Hilton Edwards. Mr. O'Hegarty had compared the Gate actors unfavourably with the Abbey company. 'At the moment,' writes Hilton, 'we get more than our share of cold water from the critics who seem curiously chary of attacking the Abbey. But we understand their feelings; we are young, we are struggling and at the moment we are merely promising. We boast no academic distinction, we have no Celtic Renaissance behind us. In fact we are a bunch of upstarts uncomfortably progressive and intensely alive.' That was Hilton in top form, a central heating plant in himself.

Seán O'Faolain obliged with a stunning piece on provincialism. The opening sentences are truly majestic: 'Provincial being one of those words which, with the passage of time, have acquired fresh connotations — in this case pejorative — it is impossible to use it now without some attempt at a fresh definition.' He attacks the Irish reading public and with reason; 'The lack of valuable criticism is as devastating as the locust. There is a total lack of interest in the young writer and he finds no outer stimulus whatever.' O'Faolain goes on to say: 'Under such circumstances it is natural that the Irish writer ignored or misunderstood at home would gravitate away from his own people — often in bitterness and disgust even though he knows at the same time that all his interests and sympathies are forever anchored deeply and firmly in their lives ... this revulsion-attraction complex has had a profound effect on Irish literature.' O'Faolain lists the exiles, Pádraic Colum, George Moore, Kate O'Brien, L. A. G. Strong, James Joyce and the young Yeats 'rushing between London and Dublin'. He concludes: 'it is that native provincialism gripping those who have remained at home which has produced the happy patriots.'

This article was written in August 1932. Well I suppose things have improved since then, though a nation which claps a tax on books, including school text books can hardly be described as highly civilised. Still, a number of novelists and poets have emerged over the years and triumphed, in spite of the provincialism which, in part, was the result of the despotic censorship imposed by the Church. 'The happy patriots', charming phrase, have gone with the windbags.

A fellow calling himself E. W. Tocher contributed an article 'Towards a Dynamic Theatre'. He turned out to be the Gate's star dramatist, Denis Johnston, and this was a highly explosive piece of work: 'In conclusion the salvation of theatre rests with the dramatists — the only people connected with the stage today who are consistently lagging behind (this was in the April/May *Motley* 1933) and the dramatist must be prepared to go ahead and make gallant fools of themselves without any regard for crashing barrage of heavy criticism that will be put down practically by all the London newspaper men. It is these tiresome old gentlemen who are contributing towards the slow murder of the theatre as an institution.' Brave words written so long ago.

In order to recoup *Motley's* bank balance which was nil — the debts were always paid by generous Edward Longford but even his purse began to give out — we decided to put on a one night revue called *Motley Medley*. Needless to say it was instantly retitled *Motley Muddley*. My memories of it are vague as indeed was the production. I do remember Harry Fine, a fellow of infinite vitality, giving an imitation of Hilton Edwards which consisted of violent audience involvement and a great deal of shouting. I can still see in the mind's eye, which is all that is left, the two De Vere White brothers, Dr. Bob Collis, and my brother John hammering up wooden boxes which were, I think, meant to express expressionism. Everyone gave imitations of themselves, some larger than life. Two skits were banned at the last minute because they might be offensive to the Abbey Theatre which was odd after Hilton's attack on the critics for not being critical enough of the Abbey. These banned skits consisted of masked dancers wearing long winter underwear and go-loshes, beating drums and uttering strange unintelligible speeches. The other day I was watching the Krishna ensemble performing near the gates of Stephen's Green and was, I fear, irresistibly reminded of the *Plays for Dancers*. The audience for *Muddley* was large and enthusiastic mainly because their participation was total.

I kept up with my Gate companions over the years I lived in the USA. I remember lunching at the Ritz in Boston with Hilton during the time he was going through hell with the production of *Cass Maguire*. 'Ruth Gordon is being so difficult, dear, life is one long ulcerated stomach ache.' Micheál stayed with me in Cambridge while he was performing in a production of *Much Ado About Nothing*, with Margaret Leighton and John Gielgud. The theatre was radical-chic, newly built on the banks of the Charles river. A great part of the time it seemed to be right in the river and much ado was caused by the rat problem. Later, Micheál stayed with us while he was presenting his triumphant one-man *Oscar* in Boston. Of course he was feted by the American Irish in south Boston and returned from one shamrock soirée a wreck: 'I've been among savages, dear. Give me some hot milk.' He came over again for the Irish Arts Festival with his other one-man show *I Must be Talking to My Friends*. Micheál talking to taxi drivers was another thing. I've a vivid memory of him in a blinding snowstorm stepping into a taxi in Cambridge, Mass., and saying to the astounded driver: 'Take me to the North Pole, darling, and fast!'

My correspondent from Paris was Owen Sheefy Skeffington and he covered films and theatre and nobody could have been better. W. J. K. Mandy (Jimmy) and George Hetherington wrote from London and they are still informative and amusing to read. I was very proud of my poets. John Betjeman sent me a chic piece of verse about an Irish castle. Charlie Donnelly who died in the Spanish war sent me a lovely little short poem called 'In a Library'. Donogh McDonogh also contributed and so did Patrick McDonough who also died young and whose poetry was unappreciated and should be brought out again. There were some excellent translations from the Russian by Blanaid Salkeld and trans-lations from the Spanish by Ethna McCarthy. Other poets included Niall Sheridan, Irene Haugh and John Lane. The latter was discovered by Frank O'Connor. Very few poets could get published then and even *Motley* with its small circulation and lack of monetary recompense was a welcome outlet. But everything centred around the Gate Theatre for me and for many others. It had a magic lure for youthful talent. The Drama League which preceded it was too amateur and too cliquey. It was run by the intellectual elite and though the productions were inter-esting and stimulating, it was primarily for the Few. I think Christine Longford summed it all up most succinctly in February 1933. She wrote:

'The Gate is not a little theatre where high-brow plays are recited by a chosen few, but a real theatre in a capital city where the play, the acting and the production combine to make the final harmony which is called a show. No show is allowed to go on in which any element is neglected. Hilton Edwards is a producer who is never satisfied with the second best. He extracts the last drop of significance from a play and the last ounce of activity from his actors and conducts his cast like the conductor of an orchestra. That is why the Gate is Dublin's theatre of the nineteen-thirties. Now that the little theatres of the world have done their best and are dropping into bankruptcy and the commercial theatre has done its worst and is making a belated search for fresh plays, the Gate retains its balance and is going straight ahead.'

Very few group movements in the Arts last very long. They are like the months of spring with the darling buds of May bursting into summer and then slowly they decline into winter and there is never a second spring. The best years of the Gate lasted the six or seven years before 'the split', when we were all united in a common cause. There was a freshness, a joyousness about it which matched the spring of our own years when the writers, the directors, the actors and the designers all merged together in perfect unison. And so began the one and only, the exciting and original Gate Theatre of Dublin. For a few golden years this theatre gave me moments of ecstatic achievement and intellectual creativity which I've never known again. Was it really all that beautiful or does the distance in time embellish one's memories with a rosy glow? Why do I remember the irrelevancies far more clearly than the relevancies? Why do I see Mrs. Carmichael dispensing coffee in the foyer as if she wished it were hemlock! I can see the back of Edward Long-ford's head, seated in the front row of the theatre, and hear his delighted chuckles. I can hear Orson Welles appalled shout when I read the cards for him and assured him he would be an immensely successful stock-broker.

Alas and alack, so many of the original cast of *Youth's the Season—?* are dead. And now our dear Micheál has left us. I think something died in us all when we stood in that graveyard on the sloping hillside in Howth. The waters of Dublin Bay glimmered in the cold sun-shine; the Wicklow mountains were outlined against the bleak, blue, wintry sky. The seagulls screamed mournfully over our heads while the coffin was lowered into the grave as if voicing the inner anguish of the friends who stood silently watching Micheál's final exit. Most of all one mourned for the living, for the friend and partner of fifty years who could not restrain his tears when Paddy Bedford plucked a green car-nation from the funeral wreath and placed it in Hilton's buttonhole. Yes, something in us died with Micheál Mac Liammóir, something which was part of our lives too. One thinks of his wit, his irrepressible youthful-ness, his enthusiasms, his versatility as painter, designer, actor, and writer. How we will miss his conversations, the mimicries, the malice, the naughtiness, the impudence, and all in several languages! The last time I saw him it was in hospital. He whispered, 'there's nothing to be said for old age, Mary?' I said: 'Nothing, Micheál, nothing.' And then he whispered again: 'You wouldn't put a question mark after *Youth's the Season* now, Mary?' I took his hand and said: 'No, Micheál, no.'

GABRIEL FALLON

author, drama critic and former member of the board of directors
of the Abbey Theatre

On 22 November 1928, Lady Gregory wrote in her *Journal*: 'I stayed on at the Abbey and had tea at a cafe and went into the Gate Theatre performance at the Peacock. It was *Diarmuid and Grania* by Micheál Mac Liammóir—beautifully staged and lighted; no plot, just the simple story of Finn and the lovers. Simple language, a straight story, very moving. It had been given in Irish in Galway and had been very successful there. A new departure. I felt far more in sympathy with it than with *The Big House* at the Abbey, going on next door.'

And so well she might; for it reminded her of the ideals which inspired herself and Yeats when they set out 'to bring upon the stage', as they put it, 'the deeper thoughts and emotions of Ireland'. They were to learn in time that the thoughts and emotions of Ireland were not as deep as they had imagined them to be. For all that, she alone stood by their foundation, on the principle, as she once said to me, that '*Grip* is a good dog; but *Hold Fast* is a better!' In 1919 Yeats had written her an open letter protesting against the Abbey's commonplace realism and saying: 'We did not set out to create this sort of theatre, and its success has been to me a discouragement and a defeat.'

Until the publication of her autobiography (the work is in the hands of my good friend Colin Smythe) we shall not know if Lady Gregory saw any other production by these talented men of the theatre, Hilton Edwards and Micheál Mac Liammóir, founders of the Dublin Gate Theatre Productions, which came to birth in 1928, in the tiny 101-seat Peacock Theatre attached to the old Abbey with an entrance from the street of that name. It had been designed from a front and back Georgian drawing-room by my good friend Dr. Micheal Scott, actor and architect, as a possible 'experimental' theatre for the Abbey; or, as Yeats is reported to have said, 'in order to let the Government see that we were doing something with the monetary grant that they had given and would continue to give us.'

*   *   *

That first 1928 season at the Peacock will live in the memory of all who love the theatre *qua* theatre; and not merely Mrs. Soandso's kitchen or Mr. Whatyehmacallim's sitting-room, with one wall down! And so much can be said for the second 1929 season in that place. Poverty ruled the roost. There was no great rush of audiences to the Peacock. But there was instead a handful of helpful and loyal friends who stuck by the partners through thick and thin. Hilton Edwards and Micheál Mac Liammóir, just like the rest of us, had to live; but they were not interested in money.

After all, Micheál might make a few paltry pounds from writing or illustrating a book in Irish; or he might sell a picture or two, for say, a guinea; or, very well then, two guineas, if the purchaser generously insisted. Hilton could sing between films at the cine-variety sessions in the Corinthian. (I am not likely to forget his rendering of *The Blind Ploughman* at that place. Nor indeed was Barry Fitzgerald as we rested there between the Abbey's matinee and night show on a hot Saturday afternoon.) And who remembers the singing (and dancing) of both partners when they appeared in a 'Gipsy Song Scena' at the Capitol?

Those who to-day think in terms of an elegant house in Harcourt Terrace ought to be reminded that were it not for the shrewd acumen of their one-time business manager, the late but unforgettable Bill Ryan, they mightn't have had a roof over their heads. Of these two memorable seasons at the Peacock one could be certain that if at the end of a week the partners had a fiver to split between them the attendance must have topped the seventy per cent mark. Many years later, finding Yeats in one of his expansive moods I tempted him to talk about the Abbey's early financial difficulties. I shall never forget his concluding remark: 'As often as not, Fallon,' he said, 'poverty is the mother of genius.' It certainly was in the case of the two partners at the Peacock. And let this be accounted to them for virtue; that never in the course of a long career, during which poverty was, as often as not, just around the corner, did they lend their names or their personalities to the base purposes of commercial advertising.

*   *   *

Rather than listing the names of their successes at the Peacock and after, let us ask what it was that they set out to do, and what it was that urged them to do it. First of all, let Micheál speak. He is musing upon a holiday spent by himself and his partner in Berlin in 1931:

> Every night we were at the theatre and I think I learned more about design that summer than ever before. It was Berlin with its Russian influences that taught me how unnecessary the British fetish of the customary masking-in was becoming, Berlin that broke up my growing obsession with Playfair's symmetry, that freed my brain from a thousand microscopic tyrannies of visual convention. And yet Berlin had its own fetishes of solidity and heavy representationalism, and as I watched the architectural magnificence of the Volksbuhne and Deutsches Theater productions I began to wonder if the same splendour could not be achieved with a lighter and more suggestive method.

And now Hilton: musing upon his own very personal ideal:

> I wish I could see a new form, a sort of Elizabethanism, a simplicity — you don't know how I've grown to hate painted canvas, wooden structures, a half-hearted attempt to create an impossible illusion that when it's most successful is only a mirror of the commonplace. I believe in the direct contact, the taking of the audience into one's confidence, a sort of music-hall intimacy. 'Come down to me here, I've something to tell you.' That's how Shakespeare wrote, I'm certain of it. '*You who are mute and audience to this act*' — that *you* means the audience, you see. '*had I but time as this fell sergeant death*
>
> > *Is swift in his arrest*
> > *O, I could tell you. . . .*'

See the thrill? Contact, you see; the audience becoming part of the play, *assisting*, isn't that what the French call it?

And now Micheál again:

> Yeats is worn out and the Abbey has come to mean something he had never planned; our own theatre is already groping its way through a mire of public indifference and conventional interior neurosis, the muddy reaction of varying talents that can find no existing standard by which they might be measured. But we have proved that we are not afraid of work and poverty, and who shall tell but that the spade will hit something more than a stone one day and the magical fluid spring forth and our corrupted weary faces be filled with light?

In these quotations one can detect echoes of the faded hopes of Augusta Gregory and William Butler Yeats; the former with her insistence on the co-operation of the three A's, which she outlined in her speech on 27 December 1925, the Abbey Theatre's twenty-first birthday. 'In the theatre,' she said, 'we have the three A's, interdependent, inseparable: Author, Actor, Audience. We are necessary to one another. If these three hold together, I hope the Abbey will last into the far future and leave a fine tradition (and here she quoted from Yeats's *The Golden Helmet*: *'That the long-remembering harpers have matter for their song'*). Hence the pleasure she derived almost exactly three years later from Hilton's production of Micheál's *Diarmuid and Grania* at the Peacock.

Yeats, too, saw in the new departure his hope that words would be restored to their original sovereignty; for, as he put it, with good reason and not a little bitterness:

> *But actors lacking music*
> *Do most excite my spleen*
> *They say it is more human*
> *To shuffle grunt and groan*
> *Not knowing what unearthly stuff*
> *Rounds a mighty scene.*

The founders of the Dublin Gate Theatre were not to disappoint the hopes of their forerunners.

*   *   *

At the end of their unforgettable season at the Peacock they moved to more commodious premises at the Rotunda on Parnell Square where, what was formerly known as the 'Upper Concert Hall' was converted, with some assistance from Michael Scott, to suit the more demanding exigencies of theatre. In December 1929, with the help of a Board of well-wishing Directors, the Dublin Gate Theatre Company Limited was formed and registered. Within twelve months it had reached a financial crisis!

In December 1930 one of their staunchest supporters, Lord Longford, generously came to their assistance and in the summer of 1931 became a Director and eventually Chairman of the Board. They began to learn the lesson that art — great art — seldom produces dividends, at least so far as Dublin is concerned.

They opened at the Rotunda with a production of Goethe's *Faust* and staged works by Georg Kaiser, Merejkowski, Strindberg, Wiers

Jensen, Martinez Sierra and Herman Ould. They gave the first production of Micheál Mac Liammóir's *Easter 1916* which they were destined to revive many times; presented Shakespeare's *The Merchant of Venice*; staged Shaw's *Back to Methuselah* (in its entirety!) as well as a number of other plays by Irish authors—Farquhar, St. John Ervine, Ulick Burke, Austin Clarke and T. C. Murray amongst them. They even lightened their repertoire with the uproarious *Ten Nights in a Bar Room* and presented their first 'International Variety Entertainment' — *Christmas Pie*. They even tried a 'send up' presentation of the old melodrama *Sweeney Todd (The Demon Barber)*. Yet for all that they were to find themselves in the red, were it not for the financial generosity afforded by Lord Longford.

Of their Fifth Season (Third at the Rotunda) during which Lord Longford blossomed forth as a dramatist, I intend to refer to one production only — Shakespeare's *Hamlet*. I have seen good Hamlets and bad Hamlets in my time but this is one that within two months of my eightieth year still remains alive in my memory. I refer of course to Micheál Mac Liammóir's Prince of Denmark in a production so ably directed by Hilton Edwards. I note that in my *Irish Monthly* review of it I referred to it as 'A More than Memorable Hamlet'. It was all that, as much for Micheál's design as for Hilton's production. I note, too, that I referred to Micheál's conception of the character as William Hazlett's Hamlet. Hazlett held that no play suffered so much in being transferred to the stage. And, Heaven knows, that is only too true even to-day. Consider Olivier's Hamlet whether on stage or screen: a voice in vacuo, a face without a heart. 'Hamlet himself,' wrote Hazlett, 'seems hardly capable of being acted.' And for this he laid down his definition of the character.

And now I quote from the *Irish Monthly*. 'To every point of Hazlett's definition Mr. Mac Liammóir's conception conformed. For here was a Hamlet wrapped up in his own reflections, *thinking aloud*. Here was a Hamlet who made no attempt to impress his words upon others by a studied exaggeration of emphasis or manner. A Hamlet who did not *talk at* his hearers. There was much (very much) of the gentleman and the scholar in him; and perhaps a shade — just a shade — too little of the actor. A pensive air of sadness sat — and sat reluctantly — upon his brow, but no appearance of fixed and sullen gloom. Weakness and melancholy were there, but harshness was not. Inevitably, the most amiable of misanthropes. This Hamlet walked and spoke gracefully within the play, nor did he at any time, as many of his fellows do, straddle the footlights to split the ears of the groundlings. He was not, as some are, a walking neurosis, nor yet an actor wallowing in a great part.'

I vividly recall that moment when his partner, that master of position and movement, had Micheál stand at a pillar, his handsome head tilted slightly backward against (presumably) the cold stone, moving ever so slowly and wearily from side to side as he spoke the great soliloquy beginning: 'O, that this too too solid flesh, etc.' When he came to the words: '*How, weary, stale, flat and unprofitable seem to me the uses of this world*' he made every soul in his audience feel as he felt. Of course, being a critic I had a few faults to find. I would have liked more fire on the line '*This is I, Hamlet the Dane*', more withering scorn and sarcasm in the recorder's scene. But against these faults I was compelled to measure the immense depth of feeling in his '*I loved Ophelia; forty thousand brothers could not with all their quality of love make up my sum.*'

I cannot say if Yeats saw this performance. I feel he would have loved it if he did; for from the age of twelve when his father, great painter and sound philosopher (the family then living in Bedford Park, Chiswick) brought him to see Irving's *Hamlet*, the character entered the schoolboy's soul and dominated it for the rest of his life. He resolved he would wear the mask that Irving's Hamlet revealed. Much to his father's disgust the boy seemed to have no eyes for the beautiful Ellen Terry. Yeats would have loved the sense of poetry that Micheál's Hamlet revealed, confirming the fact that some actors were still not 'lacking music'.

44

*   *   *

It seems to me that it would be fruitless at this point to usurp the function of the historian and to attempt to set out in detail all that followed that Fifth Season at the Rotunda premises except to pay tribute to their faithfulness to that greatest of all playwrights — William Shakespeare. Whatever exigencies of circumstances they found themselves in — and bankruptcy faced them on a number of occasions — they made him the lynch pin of their theatrical career, with a magnificence of costume and décor, in which they were aided by the work of Mollie McEwen, and later by that naturally-talented genius, Michael O'Herlihy (now directing films in Hollywood). The glories of their foreign tours, Cairo, Alexandria, Malta, Athens, Ljubljana, Zagreb, Belgrade, Salonica, Sofia, Bucharest, (not forgetting Cork, Belfast and Cardiff) were offset by the break with Lord Longford (a link that could never have held) and by poor box-office takings at home.

February 1940 found them at Dublin's Gaiety Theatre facing a management which was unashamedly 'commercial'. For Louis Elliman (who in the course of time became one of my closest friends) the thing that mattered most in the theatre was *the box-office*. In Hilton and Micheál he undoubtedly had a problem to deal with. He tried hard but failed; and Shakespeare, not to mention lesser 'art' works, went on whether he liked it or not. There is a story not generally known which ought to be told here. When Micheál had written his *magnus opus The Importance of Being Oscar* he wisely recorded it. The partners played it for Louis and suggested it should be given a trial. To say that Louis was horrified at the suggestion is to put it mildly. Time passed and a Dublin Theatre Festival came along. Louis was in a quandary as to what the Gaiety should present. The boys suggested *The Importance*. Knowing that with a subvention he might be reasonably safe in taking a chance Louis agreed to a week's run. From the first night on, the Gaiety was packed and *The Importance* was voted the artistic success of the Festival!

A season later Louis suggested that it mightn't be a bad idea to do a week's revival of *The Importance*. It ran for six standing-room-only weeks! At the end of that run Micheál was obviously exhausted. On the final night Louis and his charming wife Ettie had a little surprise for Micheál. They had asked me to arrange a kind of 'This is Your Life' show and to bring on stage at the final curtain (there were seven in all) a group of distinguished Irishmen who had known and admired Micheál.

I was to do so under the title: 'An Oscar for an Oscar!' (so like Louis!) All this I did; and what surprised me even more than the magnificent tributes paid to him, was (a) the genuine humility of the victim, to whom at the close I handed a mignificent specimen of Waterford glass; and (b) not a single person left that crowded house though it was at least forty minutes after the last bus had departed!

The affection in which President de Valera and his good wife Sinéad held Micheál and the work of the Partners is fairly well known. What is not so well known is that at one time in their career Eamon de Valera, acting through the then Minister for Posts and Telegraphs, Patrick J. Little, (who was a kind of one-man Arts Council for the government) offered to buy the Queen's Theatre for the partners who would be expected to run it as a 'kind of Irish Old Vic' (ridiculous phrase!). For some reason, best known to Hilton and Micheál — and to God — the offer was refused. While on this subject I feel I ought to mention that Gerard Fay in *Fay's Third Book*, who was an honoured guest at the laying of the new Abbey's foundation stone has something interesting to say about Micheál. But first of all something about the stone itself. Ernest Blythe, manager and director of the Abbey, wouldn't hear of the name of Annie F. Horniman appearing on it. 'She hated Ireland and the Irish' was his verdict. Well, she certainly hated Willie Fay and forced this situation to such an extent that Willie was compelled to leave the Abbey. His brother Frank sadly left with him.

But when Mr. B. flatly declared that the name of the Fays would not appear on the stone, I decided to go into action. I wrote to Gerard Fay whom I had known from his school-boy days onwards and told him that if Mr. B. got his way I would resign from the Board of the Abbey Theatre and widely publicise my reasons for doing so. Gerard wrote to his cousin in the Department of External Affairs and informed him of the situation. Within a fortnight Mr. Blythe glumly informed the Board that the Department of External Affairs wanted the names of the Fays to appear. He lamely added that someone must have written to the Department. Well, I, for one, could lay my hand on my heart and say that I hadn't!

When the stone was being laid Micheál was ill in hospital and was visited there by President de Valera. Gerard then records that he was told that Micheál Mac Liammóir was to become managing-director of the Abbey Theatre in the place of Ernest Blythe, who would announce his retirement at the end of the official luncheon. That didn't happen, of course. But at the heart of every rumour there is always an element of truth; and my knowledge of Mr. Blythe, garnered during my fifteen *fighting* years as a Director of the Abbey Theatre, leads me to believe that there may well have been some deep-seated political intrigue at work which frustrated the proposed appointment, one which would have met with the whole-hearted approval of President de Valera. Within a few weeks of the opening of the new Abbey I put forward the suggestion (not knowing anything about the above) that the National Theatre might effectively be shared between the Abbey (pursuing its own way) and Hilton and Micheál pursuing theirs. Mr. Blythe made it quite clear that such an idea was a preposterous one; and one to be quickly forgotten.

Was it so? There is a passage in the Epilogue to the second edition of Micheál's *All for Hecuba*, that has always made me think deeply, and then blush. Here it is: 'One day about a year ago, remembering that it was I, during the Longford split as our quarrels in 1937 have been called, who suggested the sharing of the Gate Theatre building between Edward Longford's company and our own, each taking six months, the thought of a similar scheme with the Abbey came, perhaps impertinently, into my head. This was founded upon the certainty that, after the burning of the old Abbey Theatre — and the natural focussing of the lights of Government and Arts Council aid upon its needs, any financial help for the Gate, by which I meant Hilton and myself, was improbable. Also it came from the knowledge that after the lamented death of Lennox Robinson there was a good deal of semi- official talk of my being offered a directorship of the Abbey.' (Now let us pause here.)

I did not know until a year or so ago that the second edition of Micheál's fascinating book had an Epilogue. Had I been in possession of the above information I would undoubtedly have used some fox's trick (political or otherwise), just as I did with the names of the Fays, to bring this much desired consummation about. Mr. Blythe's refusal even to discuss the matter was not the only occasion on which I had reason to suspect that I was allowing myself to be fooled. Now mark what immediately follows the passage quoted above: 'I did not welcome that notion; and I was delighted that a far more suitable man than I, Gabriel Fallon, the critic and writer on the Theatre, had been invited.' Micheál, dear shade, I have frequently asked the Lord to accept your humility in reparation for that *gaffe* of 'a far more suitable man!' Indeed, it was to shut my mouth as a critic and to paralyse my hand as a writer on the Theatre that Mr. B. so readily assented to my appointment to the Board. And I have evidence enough to prove it.

*　　　*　　　*

'Alas, 'tis true, I have gone here and there and made myself a motley to the view.' But what is far worse, and was possibly so in Shakespeare's eyes, I, God help me, was a drama critic! And there were times, many times, when I clashed with the Gate Theatre. Indeed, on some occasions swords were out on both sides. But they never barred me from their presentations. It was left to Lord Longford to do that; and to warmly — indeed flatteringly — welcome me back again! But I never failed to respect the integrity of these two superb artists of the theatre, even in the midst of our disagreements; and they, in their turn, came to respect mine. And when that good friend of the arts, Charles Haughey, came at length to their assistance, I was amongst the first to cheer. If I have said once that Ireland's theatre owes a debt to Hilton Edwards and the late lamented Micheál Mac Liammóir that it can never repay, I must have said it a dozen times. But I have not the slightest hesitation in saying so again. Let the Abbey do what it will, these two men have done what the Abbey could never do; down through the long years they have shown us what the theatre really is, and what it has the potentiality of being. I am glad to note that to-day's generation is packing in to see *Equus* at the Gate. I have not gone; it would not be my kind of play, mainly because I love all animals (second only to little children). And, anyway, even when I pass the theatre in a bus, the ghost of the years long gone haunt me with the reminder that my own long day is drawing to a close.

JOHN JORDAN
author, literary and drama critic and broadcaster

When the time comes to write the official history of the Gate Theatre the historian may have some difficulty in disentangling the hard facts of the Theatre's first lustrum. My asseveration is itself based on a hard fact. When in 1946, Micheál Mac Liammóir published his first autobiographical book, *All For Hecuba*, he gave a reasonably accurate account of those years, including the arrival on the scene, at a crucial stage, of Edward, Sixth Earl of Longford (1902–1961). But some thirty years later than Mac Liammóir's book, an RTE television documentary, in which Mac Liammóir, Dr. Hilton Edwards and Christine, Countess of Longford, all took part, presented the facts crazily out of focus, and so far as I know, no-one cared enough or knew enough to put the record straight.

If I try to do so now, it is in the interests of factual truth and not out of partisanship. My guideline is a rare little brochure published in 1940, just twelve years after the foundation of the Gate (at the Peacock, as the Dublin Gate Theatre Studio), and only four after the first visit to Egypt of Edwards and Mac Liammóir, which precipitated the 'split' with Lord Longford. Before going on to the years of what Mac Liammóir was to call 'the Longford regime', it may be useful to set the scene.

It should be remembered that those two astonishing seasons at the Peacock, which housed a capacity audience of one hundred-and-one — which meant, if we exclude 'paper', that over a two-week run 1,200 people would be the maximum to see a single production — brought the partners (and their co-directors, the late Madame D. Bannard Cogley and the late Gearóid O Lochlainn) only into the late spring of 1929. But the partners were not idle for the rest of the year: apart from continuing his association as producer with Taibhdhearc na Gaillimhe, Micheál played at the Abbey in Lennox Robinson's *Ever the Twain*, and wrote the Civic Week pageant *The Ford of the Hurdles*, which Hilton directed in the Mansion House. (For the rest of this piece, I am dropping formalities.) The text of this pageant has not been published but one of the original players, the late Art O'Murnaghan, deposited a typed copy in the National Library.

But all of this activity was merely marking time before the inauguration of the Gate Theatre. On Christmas Eve, 1929, the Dublin Gate Theatre Company Limited was registered, and on 17 February 1930, the Gate Theatre was opened, with the *Faust* of Goethe (perhaps an inauspicious choice in the short-term view). There were two new Directors, the late Gordon Campbell, who was to become Lord Glenavy, and the late Norman Reddin.

By the end of the year, the Company was in financial difficulties. It was then, in December 1930, that Edward Longford saved the company by taking up the remaining three hundred shares. By the following summer he was himself a director, and eventually, Denis Johnston became another. My little brochure gives no clue as to when O'Lochlainn and Madame Cogley disappeared from the Board, nor Gordon Campbell nor Norman Reddin. What is incontestable is that the association with Edward Longford lasted for five years, from the end of 1930 to the end of 1935, embracing six Dublin seasons, and a brief London season in June 1935.

Before going on to the 'split', it is only fair to record that the Longfords, Edward and Christine, made valuable contributions to what we may call the Gate's dramatic literature: notably their joint translation of the *Orestia* of Aeschylus, Christine's Anglo-Irish comedy, *Mr. Jiggins of Jigginstown* and indisputably, Edward's play about Swift, *Yahoo*, which by all accounts provided Hilton with a magnificent vehicle. This was one of the offerings during the London season of June 1935.

Towards the end of that year Hilton and Micheál accepted an invitation from the Egyptian Government to visit Cairo and Alexandria. Edward was against the idea, on the ostensible grounds that their main preoccupation should be with Dublin. I have never discussed the matter with any of the principals concerned, but it has often occurred to me that Edward, not quite thirty-three when he made the portentous decision, may have done so on ideological grounds: the nationalist and anti-colonialist flames may still have been burning bright. Certainly, as late as 1947, I heard him dismiss Virgil as an imperialist.

Whatever the grounds for Edward's objections, Hilton and Micheál brought a company to Egypt where they played during March-April 1936. While there they learned that Edward had formed a 'Dublin Gate Theatre' Company and was playing in London. Clearly, the position had become intolerable.

When Hilton and Micheál returned to Dublin, they found it impossible to reconcile their differences with Edward. The Dublin Gate Theatre Company Ltd. ceased to function as a theatrical unit. There emerged Longford Productions and Dublin Gate Theatre Productions. And so, for the season 1936–37, Edwards and Mac Liammóir first operated as an independent management under the name Dublin Gate Theatre Productions.

Speculation as to how the Theatre might have developed, had there not been a 'split', up to quite recently has been an agreeable, if not passionate, topic of chat among amateur historians of the theatre. Most of my contemporaries incline to the view that the 'split' was a good thing: if only because the Dublin theatrical repertory was augmented.

But the Longford connection never really vanished. In 1946, for instance, it was Edward's version of *Oedipus Rex* that Hilton directed at the Gaiety (with Anew McMaster as Oedipus). As late as 1957, the two managements in a sense came together for the Dublin Theatre Festival to present Micheál's last Robert Emmet in *The Old Lady Says 'No!'*. Nor can I forget a post-card from Micheál in Rome in 1947 to Christine in Dublin: 'Rome more wonderful than ever. Wish you were here to tell me the truth about it all.' Clearly the *camaraderie* of that early lustrum of the Longford regime had not wholly evaporated.

DENIS JOHNSTON

playwright, author and former member of the board of directors
of the Dublin Gate Theatre

The last couple of years of the 'twenties was not a very inspiring era in Dublin's theatrical history. We were enjoying, of course, a regular supply of amusing witchen comedies by Brinsley Macnamara and George Shiels directed by Lennox Robinson with a familiar cast, and there was a new School of Ballet with choreography by Ninette de Valois. But Paul Vincent Carroll or Miss Deevy had not yet appeared, while O'Casey had taken himself off in a rage to the larger world of Shaftesbury Avenue and was threatening never to return. During the winter months we also had the performances of the Drama League supplemented by its offspring, the New Players, who had been operating for some time past in the hundred-and-two seater 'Peacock', perched between the back of the Abbey pit and the roar of Lower Abbey Street.

There was also a number of peripheral groups — Mary Manning's 'Anomalies' and John Lodwick's 'Stage Society', and an occasional production by Madam Kirkwood Hackett and the poet, Lyle Donaghy. This last took place in the Mansion House where, on one remarkable evening, a heavy chandelier fell with a crash upon a tableful of ancient Irish heroes during a drinking scene at Tara, one of whom was knocked out while the play gallantly continued until it came to one of his lines and had of necessity to stop, while the player was brought around.

On the whole there was plenty of devoted but undisciplined acting talent, but strangely enough very little in the way of informative Direction, and even less of serious Design or Presentation. As a rule we expected to see our plays mounted in front of unrepresentative curtains probably repaired after *The Plough* disturbances, or more usually in a set of warped flats lashed together by ropes and cleats. On the other hand there was a variety of available costumes in the Abbey wardrobe ranging alphabetically from Aoibhell of the Sidhe, through the requirements of the Heffernan family to 'Uniforms' dating from *The Rising of the Moon*. And of course we were well acquainted with Doc Larchet's most competent quintet rendering *Fingal's Cave* during the gossiping Intervals.

It was into this somewhat familiar situation that two itinerants from Anew McMaster's Touring Shakespearean Company pushed their way into our ken with a seemingly ridiculous proposal to produce *Peer Gynt* — Grieg and all — on the pocket handkerchief stage of the Peacock with a cast of forty-eight—that is to say almost half the size of the entire capacity audience, leaving out of account the Press and the usual non-paying Mr. Joe Holloway. What is more, this feat was not intended to be one singular event, but was to be the opening gambit of an entirely new Theatrical Movement for Dublin. Other achievements were to follow, and we were to be the midwives assisting at this nativity.

To those of us who attended this first meeting with Hilton Edwards there was nothing new in this kind of proposition, particularly when the immediate purpose was suspected as having less to do with *Peer Gynt* than with the production of a new play by one or other of the promoters. To us sceptical listeners this was just a familiar way of getting one's own play on to some stage without the heartbreaking routine of toting it round a series of uninterested and probably illiterate Managements. One simply starts a New Theatre Movement for oneself, and stages the unborn work as second or third in the coming programme — quite a well-known and legitimate device that had previously brought Eugene O'Neill to the attention of Broadway, and might do the same for us.

Well — as we had no objection whatever to seeing *Peer Gynt* in the Peacock, a fair majority of those present were quite agreeable to lending our support to this proposal, and we listened with quiet smiles to Hilton's detailed description of how he intended to cope with Ibsen in these surroundings, regardless of what was to follow, or how long this new Movement was likely to last. We had heard much of the same kind of optimistic talk before. But the surprising difference in the present case was that we not only saw *Peer Gynt* on that pocket handkerchief stage, followed of course by Micheál Mac Liammóir's *Diarmuid and Grainne*, which Hilton had already directed in Galway in Irish without any knowledge of the language. (He was interested to find out what it was all about.) But we also found ourselves involved in the beginnings of a new Theatre that, now, fifty years later is still in existence, having in the meantime revolutionised Irish Theatrical practices, and carried its name from London through the Balkans and from Cairo to New York—which last venue has now got a Little Theatre of its own imitating the same name. (The original name came, through Hilton, from Peter Godfrey's attic playhouse of the 'twenties at the back of Covent Garden, where several of us, including O'Casey, first encountered Expressionism.)

The explanation of this success in Dublin lies, of course, in the fact that the work of Edwards and Mac Liammóir extended far beyond any expert handling of an interminable play by Ibsen, but provided our Stage with certain elements that Dublin had lacked ever since 1908, namely stylish professional Direction of works of international interest, rather than of folksey, poetical and political appeal, together with pictorial Design in Scenery, Costumes and Lighting. And — perhaps most signi- ficant of all—the personal continuity and supervision of a small resident, full-time Management.

They were egomaniacs, of course, but so much the better. These diverse requirements were everybody's wish, and by a series of sensible compromises everything managed to gell. 'The Boys' (as they were universally referred to into their sere and yellow) got the Peacock for long enough to obtain sufficient backing to enable them to expand into an annexe of the Rotunda. Hilton not only got to play Gynt, but also Shylock, Merejkowski's Tsar Paul, Wilde's Herod and Goethe's Mephis- topheles. Micheál played his own Diarmuid, Wilde's Algernon and John the Baptist, Hamlet, St. Francis of Assisi and even 'Micheál Mac Liammóir through the Ages' — the town's malicious soubriquet for his *Masque of Dublin*. While Coralie Carmicheal, their first leading lady, got Masefield's Witch—and all with considerable acclaim. I never managed to direct my own play, *The Old Lady Says No!*, but it got much more than I could ever have given it — Micheál's settings and performance together with Hilton's imaginative presentation. This quality was one of the most characteristic features of the Dublin Gate from the start — the unique ability of adding something to an Author's script that is beyond the function of a writer. Most Managements do precisely the opposite, the Moscow Art Theatre being one of the rare exceptions.

As for the Public, what it got for a pittance was O'Neill, Evreinov, Elmer Rice, Wilde, Shakespeare, Sierra, Strindberg, and the entire Orestean Trilogy, not to mention all five parts of Shaw's *Back to Methuselah* — each presented with the professional éclat that Hilton had learnt at the Old Vic and from Robert Atkins, together with the theatrical *panache* that Micheál had picked up while touring with his brother-in-law, Anew MacMaster. And all of this — to begin with — with a fine disdain for any threatening Balance Sheets. It was after a couple of seasons, when the financial side began to raise serious problems — the organisation now being a Limited Company—that the possibility of a close-down was faced at a General Meeting, and Edward, Earl of Longford, came to the rescue by announcing that he would buy all the outstanding shares, so putting the Dublin Gate back into business.

Up to this point — and indeed for some years to come — nobody connected with the Gate really expected to make a reasonable living out of the box-office takings. At the start it was not the fashionable Thing to attend these productions somewhere out on the North Side in preference to the charms of the Cinemas and the more familiar centres of commercial entertainment. The regular Theatre Buffs supported it of course, but could hardly keep it full. On the other hand, the times were fortunate in being before the advent of much interference from Unions, but there was a growing distinction between those who had to live by their theatrical employment and those who had other jobs to keep them alive. This tended to bring the matter of payment to a head, as had proved to be the case in the revived Drama League, which went down with a crash in about 1941 when everybody started to demand to be paid. This was not so much a matter of bread and butter as a question of *amour propre*. Those who did not get paid felt that they were being regarded as Amateurs, which was intolerable to some who regarded themselves as being on a level with 'Pros'. So the Drama League disappeared after a nightmare evening when half a cast refused to go on until a collection was made on its behalf. Not so in the Gate Company where rehearsals were an experience in themselves. There were rows, of course, as when Meriel Moore rang me up twice to report the startling fact that, not only had the script been thrown out of the window, but that the whole organisation had been dissolved — a matter that she felt I ought to know about.

But this was an unusual crisis, and most of the lore of the Theatre centres around amusing stories of events during rehearsal. Unlike the Abbey, when the inevitable split came along, it was not a split in the Acting Company but only in the Management. There was no victim-isation or setting up of dissidents in other premises, with conflicting appeals to the Public. The only non-theatrical nastiness concerned the Corporation whose Inspector was disturbed by the fact that the Lavatory Doors distinguished between the sexes only in the National language, which he felt might cause confusion amongst visitors from abroad. Micheál's reply to what he considered to be interference with his decor was to add the words on these doors not only in English, but also in French, German, Italian, Spanish and finally in Chinese. Whatever the Corporation may have felt about this, for a considerable time afterwards the Theatre was harassed by a series of requirements concerned with

Fire Hazards and other constructional details that were attributed to some annoyance over Micheál's riposte. On the other hand the Government itself has since expressed its approval of both Gate and Abbey with most generous Grants-in-Aid which have ended most financial troubles, and may be seen reflected in the size of the Staff Lists on contemporary Programmes, when compared with what they used to be in older — and perhaps happier days.

As it is, the personel still chuckles over tales such as the final Dress Rehearsal of *Romeo and Juliet* when the same Meriel appeared at an upper window of the Capulet residence, and — instead of the line: Wherefore art thou Romeo? — came out with the un-Shakesperean remark: 'I wish to say that if this balcony is still wobbling tomorrow night I bloody well won't appear.' There was also Hilton's criticism from the back of the Stalls to the juvenile Choristers in *The Man who Came to Dinner*: 'Boys! Boys! If there is any more of this misbehaviour tomorrow night you will remain Sopranos for the rest of your lives!' And a crisp piece of dialogue during a complicated run-through of the College Green scene in *The Old Lady Says No!*: 'Dear Diana, do try to act more like a Bus.' To which she replied rather primly: 'I was told by somebody that I am supposed to be a horse,' and got the answer 'Well you mustn't be a horse, darling. We haven't got any road sweepers.'

Amongst the Company there was for a time a young fellow who was rudely known as 'Brains', perhaps because of a practice of turning up at final word rehearsals when he had no lines to say in the play. He also had some difficulty in finding his way off stage during blackouts. Whenever the lights came up on the next scene, there would be 'Brains' still on stage trying to get off through blocked apertures or into a fireplace. When this happened once again during a final Dress Rehearsal a voice was heard to roar from the Auditorium: 'If this occurs again tomorrow night your costume will be removed and you will be thrown out into the street!' When the first performance had proceeded to this crucial point and the lights rose with no sign of 'Brains' on the stage, a sigh of relief from the cast was stilled by some tittering from the Parterre which gradually grew to a hearty laugh. The terrified Super had fled through the Audience and was now trying to creep out unnoticed by the door of the Coffee Bar.

The Dublin Gate Theatre throughout its comparatively long half century of life has experienced many problems and crises. But it has consistently stood for one fundamental principle — that it is the business of the Theatre to be theatrical. In an age of atonal music, unspeakable verse, anti-social democracy and anarchical patriotism, it is a remarkable feat to have managed to have succeeded in doing this without unintentionally flopping back into melodrama. Although one half of its original Onlie Begetters have been taken from us, it is to be hoped that it will continue to survive under the eye of the genius that has been left behind.

CHRISTINE, COUNTESS OF LONGFORD
playwright and member of the board of directors of the Dublin Gate Theatre

I wish to pay my own tribute to Hilton and Micheál. I have been their devoted admirer for fifty years and I still think of them as 'the Boys'. I shall never forget the impression they made on me when we were all young, in the year 1928. In the autumn of that year Micheál was 28, I was 27, my husband Edward Longford was 25 and Hilton at 25 was two months younger than Edward. It is only sad to remember that Micheál did not survive to celebrate his jubilee year in the Gate, and Edward has been dead since 1961. But I welcome this chance to congratulate Hilton, who is still hard at work in his theatre, and I can assure him and all the world that my admiration is undiminished.

I have been asked to write a note about Longford Productions. For the benefit of the younger generations who do not remember that company, I must explain that it was started by Edward in 1936 and ceased with his death twenty-five years later; so it lasted only half as long as Hilton's productions. In some ways I am the worst person to write about Longford shows, as I was deeply involved in them; they were part of my life and I could hardly be expected to judge them objectively. Still, as this is the jubilee year, I can trace them back to their origin in the Gate; and as I was happy to share Edward's interests, I can say something about his ideas. In the nursery (I must go back a long way), he composed, directed and acted plays, and organized his sisters, brother, cousins and little friends to present entertainments for the grown-ups. His grandmother was a severe critic and rightly insisted on the importance of audibility. 'Speak up, child' she would say when anyone muttered, and he learned that lesson early. When I first met him he had a remarkably far-reaching voice, and so I believe he had in his childhood. His sisters have told me about *Eudes, A Tragedy*, on a classical subject, in which there was a great deal of fighting, and the climax was a stage littered with corpses. It is doubtful if a script ever existed; the lines were learned in rehearsal, as in charades or in modern theatre workshops. The theme was a heroic struggle against tyranny. There must have been echoes of Eudes in *The Melians, A Tragedy*, his first play, which Hilton produced at the Gate, with Micheál playing the patriot hero.

In his teens Edward wrote *King Paulinus, A Tragedy*, in blank verse in an exercise-book which his mother preserved. The scene was Byzantine and the verse very correct, it might have been written by an eighteenth-century clergyman. The cast included 'courtiers, attendants, heralds, soldiers, populace etc.' and needless to say it was never produced, not even in the family circle, and the author preferred to forget it. The hero was called Patrick, and the same book was signed by Edward in Irish and peppered with Irish phrases from a handbook with which he was teaching himself the language at Eton. Here we may trace a juvenile interest in nationalism. He was not keen on acting at school. At his prep school he was chosen to play a girl's part in *Le Voyage de Monsieur Perrichon* and didn't enjoy it. He knew he was cast for his juvenile looks, golden curls and pink cheeks, and not for his acting ability, and it was then he decided he was no actor. At Eton he never acted, but always remembered a speech day when he first heard 'Marlowe's mighty line': two boys spoke a dialogue from *Doctor Faustus*, not in costume, just for the poetry, and years later he was proud to present *Faustus* in Longford Productions. At Oxford he didn't join a dramatic society, but as a play-goer he was madly enthusiastic, as I was. In the big commercial New Theatre we enjoyed the touring Macdona Players in Shaw; separately we applauded the Irish Players from Dublin, Máire O'Neill, Sara Allgood and Arthur Sinclair, and we hardly realised they were a 'split' from the original Abbey. On their opening night the Oxford Irish Society booked seats in the stalls and there was a mild sensation. When the theatre orchestra struck up their suitable Irish airs, 'Let Erin Remember' and so on, a crowd of young men in dinner jackets, Edward included, sprang to their feet as if for a national anthem. I didn't witness the incident, but some English and less emotional Irish thought it in very bad taste. Edward went to a party given by the company in their theatrical digs in Paradise Square, and Miss Allgood gave him a signed photograph which he treasured. Together he and I saw a touring show from the Birmingham Rep, where I had several friends, and he greatly admired the settings by Paul Shelving, the first modern décor he had ever seen in a theatre. One night I went to a party with the actors and I asked Edward to come too, but he firmly refused. He didn't know them and he hadn't a high opinion of English actors in those days. If they had been Irish or French he would have been anxious to come.

In 1923 he wrote to me from Paris that he had seen Lucien Guitry in *Tartufe*, and it was marvellous. What a lesson for hypocrites. He adored the French theatre. He sent me a picture postcard of Guitry, and on the same visit he stood for hours on the steps of the Madeleine to watch Bernhardt's funeral, though he had never seen her act. Then from Paris he went to Ireland to stay with his uncle Dunsany, who had written more plays than anyone could remember. In that house he met the famous wit Dr. Oliver Gogarty, who had written one play for the Abbey, and Lennox Robinson who had written dozens, and of course they talked about plays. Edward appreciated his uncle as a writer as well as a talker. They had a similar sense of humour, and Longford Productions in time presented *Lord Adrian, Cheezo* and *The Strange Lover. Lord Adrian* was among our earliest successes, quite brilliantly managed by our first producer Peter Powell: it was a hard play to act and to set, but well worth the trouble. A poster which looked rather snobbish announced: 'Lord Longford presents Lord Adrian by Lord Dunsany'. And in the next season Peter produced *Tartufe*, translated into English verse by Edward himself. He must have been thinking about that play for years. The verse was extremely snappy, a novelty for the Dublin audience and their reaction was splendid. The satire was perennial, he was encouraged to do more Molière, and *Tartufe* and *The School for Wives*, which was still better, remained happily in our repertory at home and on tour.

But I must go back to the nineteen-twenties. In that year '23 Edward paid his first visit to the famous Abbey and sent me a letter about it. 'The play by George Shiels,' he wrote, 'was really quite amusing, and the acting of course was excellent. There was one very funny comedian called Barry Fitzgerald.' And there was also one great disappointment: 'Miss Allgood only appeared in the intervals and sang and spoke verse, and she was so much better than anyone else, she only showed up the others. I think it was a mistake to put her into the same programme.' (Never mind, he saw her again when she played in the Gate for Hilton and Micheál.) Then in the Michaelmas Term something more important happened to us in Oxford: J. B. Fagan gave us a new theatre. It has now passed into theatrical history, but it can't be repeated too often, that the first Oxford Playhouse was a small, ugly, uncomfortable building where Fagan, the Irish actor, playwright, producer and manager worked miracles. He gave us Sophocles, Shakespeare, Congreve, Sheridan, Ibsen, Chekhov, Shaw, Wilde, Synge and Pirandello, all the plays we wanted to see, and we never missed a first night.

This was the first flush of the repertory movement, and Edward and I welcomed it as a blessing from heaven. 'Bliss was it in that dawn to be alive.' The Playhouse preached the pure gospel of the new movement; the settings were simple and quickly changed, sometimes in full view of the audience, and the curtain came down as rarely as possible; the lighting was careful, the costumes correct though not gorgeous and there was no star-billing, the company worked as a team. Among them we saw John Gielgud, Flora Robson and Veronica Turleigh when they were very young. We saw Gielgud's first performance of Valentine in *Love for Love*, and for the rest of our lives we were Congreve enthusiasts. The Playhouse gave us a liberal education in drama. At school and college we had learned something of Greek and French classics and Shakespeare, we had seen amateur shows and occasional touring companies, we had even paid flying visits from Oxford to London and Stratford; but before Fagan came, we had never enjoyed the pleasure of regular playgoing in a professional theatre. That was a prospect to which we looked forward in Ireland. And now the name of Congreve brings us nearer the Gate.

In '25 we were married and lived in Westmeath, but we went to Dublin quite often. We saw the plays of the new man O'Casey, and found them as good as their great reputation. Edward had the pleasure of seeing Barry Fitzgerald again, and the new pleasure of seeing F. J. McCormick and Eileen Crowe with him in *Juno*. We stayed a night in Dublin to see the first production of *The Plough and the Stars*, which we liked still better than *Juno*; and soon we were looking for a small house in the city, close to the trams. While we were searching, we came to another important date in our lives. In 1927, fifty-one years ago, we saw Anew McMaster and Hilton and Micheál before they saw us, because they were playing Shakespeare in Dublin. We saw McMaster's superb *Othello*, for the first time and not the last, and went back spellbound to a hotel. We had never seen such grand Shakespearean acting before, and he brought a good company to the Abbey. We certainly noticed a handsome young Cassio and a very cunning Iago. Shakespeare in the Abbey was a delight, but we didn't know, until Dubliners told us, that it wasn't a usual occurrence; McMaster was usually touring the provinces, we were lucky to see him. Twice lucky that year, we saw McMaster and found a house in Rathmines; and next year, happier still, we saw those actors, Hilton and Micheál, at work in Dublin again. In the small Peacock Theatre Hilton produced *Peer Gynt*.

In 1928 we saw the birth of the Gate in the Peacock. In 1930 we saw it re-born at its present address, and here it remains to this day, our international, un-commercial theatre of the arts. In the Gate Theatre, Parnell Square, we made friends with Hilton and Micheál. We talked about plays; both Edward and I wrote plays, and Hilton and Micheál advised us; Hilton produced our first plays, Hilton and Micheál played leading parts and allowed us to watch rehearsals. Edward joined their board of directors; and when he started his Longford Productions, from then to the end of his life he was faithful to their traditions. In Edward's name and my own I send my salutations to Hilton.

Act drop by Micheál Mac Liammóir for *Peer Gynt*, 1940 revival.

MICHEAL MAC LIAMMOIR
1899 - 1978

Hilton Edwards

Emlyn Williams

Desmond Rushe

Brendan Devlin

Richard Pine

Micheál Mac Liammóir. Photograph by Vivienne, London.

Micheál Mac Liammóir as Aleel in *The Countess Cathleen* by W. B. Yeats, 1953.

Micheál Mac Liammóir with Orson Welles in Welles' film of *Othello*, 1950.

HILTON EDWARDS

THE IMPORTANCE OF BEING OSCAR

Under this title Micheál Mac Liammóir has selected and arranged, in a chronological pattern, excerpts from the poetry, prose, letters and dramatic writings of Oscar Wilde.

By the addition of a commentary, which conceals his scholarship under a mask of comedy, he has woven a tapestry which, as he unfolds it upon the stage, reaffirms Wilde as a master of English letters and the greatest wit of his generation, and vindicates the poet's dictum that he put his genius into his life.

As the pattern emerges it reveals both the brilliance and the self-destruction of that genius; an arabesque on the plane of the highest comedy which yet hints at the underlying seriousness of Wilde's curious and dangerous philosophy. It shows him to have been aware from the first of the inevitability of his tragedy, a fate which he appears deliberately to have sought with all the perversity of his extravagant nature, and leaves no doubt that at his most triumphant moments he sensed the approach of the shadow that would at last envelop him.

There is no longer novelty in a solo performance. What gives *The Importance of Being Oscar* a unique quality is that Mac Liammóir's contribution, both as a writer and as an actor, not only confirms Wilde's stature as an artist, but relates his artistry to the now historic facts of his life; achieving what a distinguished dramatic critic has best described as: 'a new form: oral biography'.

It is as a biographer and a wit in his own right, as well as an actor, that Mac Liammóir holds the stage in this one-man *tour-de-force* which occupies, with a brief interval, something over two hours.

The success of *The Importance of Being Oscar* has been everywhere unquestioned. It was first presented in Dublin at the Gaiety Theatre as the Dublin Gate Theatre offering for the 1960 Theatre Festival, then transferred to London under the ægis of Sir Michael Redgrave and Mr. Fred Sadoff; first to the Apollo Theatre and later to the Royal Court Theatre. Both audience and press received it with enthusiasm.

An English tour was followed by a season at the Lyceum Theatre, New York, where the critical reception surpassed even London in its praise. After a tour of the United States there was an extended visit to the capitals of Latin America. At the Vieux Colombier in Paris, records were broken for that theatre. Then to Switzerland, Belgium and Holland, followed by Rome and Athens. Then a tour of South Africa followed by a still longer one to Australia and New Zealand, and short visits to Stockholm and Helsinki among other places, and various tours of England and the United States have confirmed a verdict of universal popularity and it seems that the demand for its continuance is not yet exhausted.

Actor, designer of settings and costumes, linguist and writer of plays and books both in Irish and in English, Micheál Mac Liammóir has given to the Dublin Gate Theatre, which he and I founded together in 1928, many of those qualities for which it has gained some renown, and Trinity College, Dublin, has acknowledged his contribution to Irish life by conferring on him the Honorary degree of Doctor in Laws. Mac Liammóir's range as an actor equals the variety of his talents, but he possesses a gift for which the formality of the legitimate theatre seems to afford little scope. As much as an actor he is an entertainer; a raconteur. His clouded-velvet voice, his exceptional capacity for appreciation, his gaiety and ready wit, all tend to make him a spell-binder. Whatever his skill as an interpreter of the creations of others, he seems to attain fulfilment only when juggling with ideas and words of his own selection. The *Seanachaí*, the storyteller, is a fast vanishing figure in the tradition of Gaelic and Irish culture. Oscar Wilde, though possibly unaware of it, owed much of his influence both as an artist and as a social lion to the craft of the *Seanachaí*.

Mac Liammóir also shares something of the secret of this craft. Possessing a talent so little dependent upon the complex machinery of theatrical production, it is not surprising that he was urged to the consideration of a solo performance; to seek a form that would permit him a freedom larger than that of interpretation alone.

To begin with he toyed with the idea of what might be called an anthology of Irishry: an evening of Sheridan, Goldsmith, Merriman, Shaw, Wilde, Yeats, Synge and O'Casey. He hoped to include also Denis Johnston, Joyce and other modern Irish writers, but at that time neither he nor I had discovered a way of giving form and purpose to such a varied programme.

It was when he was playing Judge Brack in *Hedda Gabler* with Peggy Ashcroft that he found in his producer, Peter Ashmore, an equally ardent student of Wilde and I believe it was Peter Ashmore's suggestion that Mac Liammóir devote his new performance to the Wilde Saga.

Mac Liammóir's interest in Wilde, his ill-starred fellow countryman, was of long standing. (At his instigation a sculptured stone plaque commemorating the centenary of Wilde's birth was placed upon the Dublin house in which he had been born.) So perhaps this was what we had been seeking; a focus upon one personality, and that an Irish writer of whom the actor had already made an extensive study.

Then came a doubt. Would an entire evening devoted to a single controversial figure of so heady a vintage be at once too limited and too cloying? Now such a doubt seems absurd: the problem soon became how to disembarrass ourselves of Wilde's riches.

We had already realised that Wilde, however wilfully he presented a premise, was seldom far from truth: that indeed his most apparently inconsequent utterance held almost invariably some deeper significance. Moreover, that everything he wrote reflected, however mistily, an aspect of his life which, in turn, was always somewhere mirrored in his writing. As above, so below. Any concept of Wilde the artist was incomplete without reference to Wilde the man; any picture of Wilde himself inadequate without comprehension of his work. With so fabulous, so gay and yet so infinitely tragic a subject, what remained for Mac Liammóir but to apply to these elements his particular philosopher's stone?

In this way *The Importance of Being Oscar* developed, not just as a recital of prose and verse, nor as a mere lecture upon the consequences of a reckless life, but as a full-length portrait in pre-Raphaelite detail, such as Wilde himself tells us was painted of Dorian Gray; a portrait that, while it showed the sitter as he appeared to the world, gave evidence of his most secret act and thought.

As the project took shape I became convinced that in performance the actor's involvement must be limited: at no moment should the actor *play*, that is to say impersonate, Oscar Wilde. He could identify himself with Wilde's theories and emotions; he could temporarily become the characters of Wilde's creation, but he must never attempt to *be* Wilde but must remain always himself. Stepping, as it were, in and out of the picture as occasion demanded he yet must always maintain an attitude aloof and ultimately objective; that of the Teller of the Story, of the *Seanachaí*. Only then, I felt certain, would he be able to establish intimacy with his audience; to forge a link between them and his subject and still be free to comment.

Further, if the performance was not to lack visual interest it must be given a shape that it could retain even after constant repetition. Something more was necessary than for the actor, just because he was alone, merely to stand or sit upon the stage or to wander as the spirit moved him.

A plan of movement must be designed that would have purpose and significance, that would defeat monotony and be both pleasing and effective. This presented problems because of the limited pattern that can be made by a single figure alone upon a stage.

Above all, everything must appear to be spontaneous, as if unrehearsed, and this effect could only be maintained consistently as the result of a planned artifice which is the reverse of chance.

Finally, what was the entertainment to look like? Where should it appear to take place? Upon an empty, curtained stage or in a set representing, for instance, a room? The first would be deadly dull, the latter too confining. So we devised a shadowy space representing no locality, furnished with the bare essentials to performance but avoiding austerity. Austerity and Wilde would surely be strange bed-fellows.

A table, a sofa, a chair and a floor covering designed to bind them together. Then (the one concession to ornament, which was also to strike the keynote to each half of the show), a pedestal on which was an urn of great waxen, moonlit lilies, a symbol at once decorative and macabre. These, for the second part of the performance, as the shadow of Nemesis crept closer, were to be replaced by autumn leaves: 'yellow and black and pale and hectic red'.

A moonlit space surrounding the gold of lamplight; a setting utterly simple and at the same time sybaritic but which commites the action to no definite locality.

The American dramatic critic, Howard Taubman, gives this impression of the first appearance on Broadway of *The Importance of Being Oscar* in a review in the *New York Times* of 15th March 1961:

'It is a virtuoso performance. . . . But even as he performs, Mr. Mac Liammóir preserves a strong measure of his own identity. . . . What he communicates is the sum of his gift as an artist and an ardent interpreter of Wilde.

'The shadows close in as the first half ends . . . when he returns the lilies in the vase have been replaced by trailing autumn leaves. Mr. Mac Liammóir himself stands in a sombre half light, his head bowed, like a man who has been through purgatory.

'Although the mood of the second part is grave, Mr. Mac Liammóir takes care to light it with flashes of Wilde's humour. . . . He does not spare Wilde nor does he judge him. He reveals him affectionately. He is an Irishman proudly proclaiming a compatriot's expression, in himself and in his work, of the spirit of Ireland. . . . Mr. Mac Liammóir has created a vivid and memorable evening in the theatre.'

Micheál Mac Liammóir in his *The Importance of Being Oscar*, 1960.

Mac Liammóir last performed *The Importance of Being Oscar* at his own Gate Theatre in Dublin for a week in December 1975 on the eve of his entering hospital for a serious operation. His performance was perhaps slower and less sparkling than previously, but had achieved a depth and intensity that was magical, and each night he received a standing ovation.

It was almost as if the audience realised the significance of the occasion: a triumphant conclusion to a brilliant career. He ended as if with an accolade.

Written as an Introduction to the published text of
The Importance of Being Oscar
by Micheál Mac Liammóir.

EMLYN WILLIAMS
actor, playwright, author

I first encountered Micheál and Hilton in the summer of 1935, in London, over midnight kippers with a mutual friend at the Criterion Restaurant. I knew Hilton was an important director, but it was the other one I was curious about for the simple reason that, while I had just opened in *Night Must Fall* at the Duchess Theatre, he had appeared a day or two later, and very successfully, in *Hamlet* at the Westminster.

For the first time he and I were conscious of each other through the two plays, which I am not comparing in any way except that both were a vehicle for the star, and that in each the star played a murderer. I had a slight pull over the other fellow, in having written my vehicle, while (rumour has it) he hadn't written his. On the other hand, while I had insisted on playing the lead in *Night Must Fall* he could — presumably — claim that he had not got *his* part through the author's influence.

I remember, leaving the Duchess to walk to the Criterion, saying to May Whitty and Angela Baddeley, 'If he's as difficult as his name, I'm in for a sticky evening.'

Hilton and I arrived pretty well at the same time and he was good company. It was half-an-hour before Micheál joined us. But he was delayed not through indifference, or even Irish dreaminess (he was no more dreamy than I am), but because the play I was in had been pruned by the author to a reasonable length, while the one he was in had not.

And when he did sail up, wearing the broadest smile ever known, I knew he was not going to be difficult. Easy. As easy as if his name had been Alfie Willmore.

I was twenty-nine; he was six years older which was of course, at that age, an enormous gap. But with Hilton's benign presence to foster conviviality we got on immediately.

What first attracted me, of course, was the outrageous and clownish sense of humour plus an unselfconsciousness which never turned into mere exhibitionism. I sensed, underneath, a shrewd cultivated intelligence capable of self-knowledge, and particularly of self-mockery. I was not to know, then, that that intelligence was also a creative one, the instrument of a gifted and eloquently personal writer: *All for Hecuba* was to be the proof of that.

Over the kippers, I was fascinated to hear that, as a child actor, he had shared a dressing-room with Noël Coward. 'We were both eleven, my dear, but the way we carried on you'd have taken us for thirty. I thought *I* was precocious till I met that one. In the same way that I assumed that I was the most flamboyant performer of my acquaintance, till I saw Mac.' Who, I gathered, was his sister's husband Anew (McMaster); and Micheál spoke of 'Mac' with a typical mixture of respect, affection and banter. 'A *marvellous* actor, starred in everything the Bard ever put to paper, bar the Sonnets and *The Rape of Lucrece*,

and I wouldn't put that past him, if he ever gets time on his hands. . . .
No, you don't have to apologise for not having heard of him, he's like me
only more so, a big fish in an Irish pond, been thrashing about in it so
hard it's got precious little water left, played every date between Kerry
and Derry. When at the top of his form, superb, once he's got the bit
between his teeth. Has, once or twice, been known to swallow it — but
a *star*! Eats, drinks and thinks *Theatre*. If ever he took up gardening
as a serious hobby you'd find the roses smelling of grease-paint, and the
lavender *reeking* of size — have *you* played *Hamlet* yet? . . . You will,
Oscar, you will. . . .'

Oscar never did, but oddly enough Micheál, not long afterwards,
after seeing *Night Must Fall* and taking a fancy to my part ('What a
juicy role, how lucky you were to have an author who was obviously
mad about you') played it in Ireland. Since I was Welsh, my devoted
author had—not unexpectedly—written the murderer as a Welshman.
'Emlyn dear, you'll be interested to hear that originally the part *must*
have been conceived as an Irishman, which is how I play it and it sounds
just right. . . .' (He had something there, for the part was later played
in the film by Robert Montgomery, with an Irish accent. And he
sounded 'just right'.)

From that night I was to know Micheál and Hilton through the years
with an affection remarkably durable considering I have never worked
with either, while our diverse activities have made continuous com-
panionship impossible: so much so, indeed, that alas I have never been
able to see any of the Gate productions being commemorated in this
book. Though I did see, in 1947 at the Vaudeville Theatre London,
Hilton's impressive production of Micheál's own charming play *Ill Met
by Moonlight*, in which M. also starred. (I had to ask him if his author
had been as mad about him as an actor, as mine had been about me.)

Then, in 1952, the bond was strengthened by my happy savouring of
Put Money In Thy Purse, Micheál's book about the filming of *Othello*
with Orson Welles. When it went out of print I lent my copy to so many
friends that it disappeared for a couple of years. It is good to know that
it has a new and thriving life as a paperback. This is a special book:
uproariously funny about the difficulties of coping with a genius loved
and maddeningly flawed, and realistic too — not mercilessly so — on
the contrary, merci*fully*: this diary proves conclusively that it is possible
to make your reader laugh without being cruel.

My copy is marked with favourite bits. Dry rot having been discovered in the Dublin house, the place 'gives forlorn appearance of set
for *King Lear* by Dali . . .: Welles, 'a bright-winged old gorilla with
almond eyes . . .': a society lady 'with a face like a golf-ball'; a masseur
'with hands like muffins': snobs 'with minds like furnished lodgings':
exquisite glimpses of Maud Gonne, of Venice, Rome, Belfast. . . . I
could go on.

Next, in April 1955 in Dublin, when I played a week of my Dickens
'Solo Performance' at the Olympia, I saw a great deal of Micheál and
Hilton; to some effect, I like to think.

By that time, in between writing a play, acting in it and in films, I
had been performing this Dickens presentation for over three years. By
the third year, I had become greedy and had started rummaging through
English literature in search of a second author to embark on. Edgar
Allan Poe? Not enough of the all-essential *variety*; not a glimmer of

humour for instance. The croak of a raven did not, somehow, promise entertainment. I did not fancy (neither, I felt, would an audience) *An Evening in a Graveyard.*

Oscar Wilde . . . of *course.* The brilliant comedy in the plays, then the poetry, then the stories, the tragedy of the trial, *De Profundis,* the *Ballad.* . . . I examined it all: rich, rich stuff. Then, over the days, I felt my excitement ebbing. The empathy I had with Dickens was not there with Wilde: I was wrong, utterly wrong for the part. Move on.

But on Dylan Thomas's death in 1953, at a charity performance I acted two of the Thomas stories and this time the unmistakable empathy was again there: so much so that I set to work to prepare a whole evening to be called *Dylan Thomas Growing Up.*

The morning after Micheál and Hilton had attended the Dickens performance, I rehearsed a complete run-through of the Thomas show, with only the two of them as audience. At lunch afterwards I could tell that Micheál had been fascinated: not necessarily by me but by the whole idea of a solo evening derived from a rich literary source — from *words.*

I said, 'Micheál, with your gift as a writer as well as ditto as actor you could prepare and do an evening!'

'Of what? Shakespeare? Synge?' he said.

'No,' I said, 'not just from plays. Plays are meant to be acted by a company — no, from a more general *literary* figure. . . .'

Then I looked at him, sitting there, slightly larger than life, exuding an exotically charming eloquence, fine words at his fingertips . . . Oscar Wilde!

I was not sure if my idea had sunk in, but several years later I felt that it had when Micheál made his resounding success with *The Importance of Being Oscar.* Talking to him just before his London opening, I congratulated him on the neatness of the title. 'Thank you, my dear — as long as one of the critics doesn't think up the headline *An Oscar of No Importance.* No critic did.

There was a sequel. Michael Redgrave, who was presenting *Oscar,* telephoned me. 'It's going wonderfully but eight minutes too long, Micheál agrees with me. It would be splendid if you could suggest tiny cuts (a sentence or a verse here and there) which would slim it down.'

With some diffidence (Micheál had been his own adaptor) I spent a week-end going through his script with a microscope, got the eight minutes out, met Micheál and explained reasons. With slight exceptions he was generously appreciative and I felt like a top surgeon who has done a good job.

Two weeks later, I talked to Michael (Redgrave) and asked how the show was going. 'Very well, but I'm afraid that since your cutting, it's running one minute longer than before you cut it!'

I rang Micheál: 'It *is* Mrs. Patrick Campbell I'm speaking to?'

'Right first time, dear, top of the class!' I said, 'Micheál, I hear it's *one minute longer.*'

'*Is* it?' A pause. '*I* know! Your cuts pulled the show together so marvellously, that the laughs are *twice* as long!'

When I told Hilton this, he said 'Now you know what it's been like to cope with an Irish Thespian.'

He coped with the Thespian, the Thespian with him, and both of them with Dublin, and Dublin with both of them, for fifty years. To the credit and pride of all concerned.

DESMOND RUSHE
journalist and drama critic

A soaring artistic temperament and a sense of solid practicality do not normally go hand-in-hand with natural compatability. But in the case of the many-splendoured Micheál Mac Liammóir, who died in Dublin on 6 March at the age of 78, they did. In him, they found a happy and fruitful blending. For not only did MacLiammóir become the colossus of Ireland's theatre scene and a significant contributor to many areas of its art and culture; he also became, in the process, a living example of practical patriotism in action.

He loved Ireland, and he expressed his love by living for it and by devoting to it, with a superabundance of generosity, the products of his remarkably fertile and diverse range of talents. His decision to do so did not spring from the heat of transient, romantic ardour. It was a deliberate, conscious choice, made at a time when the dazzle of early success might well have diverted his sights along much more glittering and financially rewarding lines. Having made his choice, he adhered to it unwaveringly.

He was born Michael Willmore in Cork, and his family moved to London when he was seven years old. Three years later, he was chosen, with Noël Coward and others, to appear in a children's play, *The Goldfish*, and an acting talent of exceptional worth was discovered. Shortly afterwards, he joined the company of the great actor-manager, Herbert Beerbohm Tree, and went on to play Oliver Twist to Tree's Fagin. By the age of twelve, he was an established child star, sharing equal billing on London theatrical posters with the giant of English theatre. Fame was his — and modest fortune, which helped sustain his rather impoverished family.

Alfred Willmore — he had adopted his father's first name for stage purposes — soon faced an inevitable and trying phase in his life, for he became too old for child roles and too young to play the juvenile, much less the adult. There was a hiatus, but with his reputation and his talent he could have confidently looked forward to a return to the London stage, with a powerfully expressive baritone voice developing to its full richness. His next acting experience was, however, to be in the Abbey Theatre on 11 December 1917. What had happened in between altered the course of his life, and resulted in the profound enrichment of Irish life.

In the autumn of 1914, he read *Ideas of Good and Evil* by the great Irish poet, William Butler Yeats, 'wading at first through the dense, mysterious pages, and later wandering through them in a rapture of joyful revelation'. That was the beginning of his Irish awakening; Yeats's pleading with all young Irish artists to turn their thoughts back to Ireland and make it 'a holy land to her own people . . . where the soul of man may be about to wed the soul of the Earth' found eager response in the imagination of the adolescent Willmore. And because Yeats had said he might have found more of Ireland if he had an adequate knowledge of the Irish language, the admiring youth took prompt action.

He sought out and joined a Gaelic League class in London, and because he had an innate linguistic gift, he made excellent progress. He spent hours in Finchley Road library combing Dineen's Irish-English dictionary so that he could expand his vocabulary, and when he eventually returned to Ireland in March, 1917, he set about achieving full fluency by going to the Irish-speaking district of Connemara.

On his first appearance in the Abbey Theatre, he had Gaelicised his name: Michael had become Micheál, and the untranslatable Willmore had become Mac Liammóir, literally son of big William. The new version would cause pronunciation problems outside Ireland, but it rolled off the tongue sonorously and well, and the transition typified the bearer's commitment to a language he would always passionately revere as the single most precious and most powerful element in recreating for Ireland a distinctive and beautiful identity.

With many others at the time, he dreamed splendid dreams, and his vision was of an Ireland at once more Gaelic and more European, more connected with the Continent in spirit and, by being bilingual, having more sympathy with other languages and other cultures. He played a practical part by writing eight books in Irish, and on every possible occasion he spoke Irish with an enchanting and expressive lilt. In later years it distressed him greatly that early hopes were not being realised and he felt, perhaps too pessimistically, that Irish would not come back as a spoken language. 'It's like a person whom you love very much and who is, you fear, inevitably dying,' he said, 'I wrote eight books in Irish because if you love someone who is dying, you cannot leave the death-bed.'

Another splendid and practical contribution Mac Liammóir made to the language was his inauguration of the Irish-speaking Galway theatre, Taibhdhearc na Gaillimhe which, like the Dublin Gate Theatre, celebrates its golden jubilee this year. The first Taibhdhearc play was his own *Diarmuid agus Gráinne*, and he made further efforts to establish Irish as a dramatic medium through his involvement with Comhar Drámaíochta, an Irish-speaking amateur company in Dublin.

During the years of absence from the stage, Mac Liammóir lived for a period with relatives in Spain; studied art at the Slade School in London; toured Europe and lived on the proceeds of his paintings — exquisitely colourful works which showed a pronounced Aubrey Beardsley influence. He could have made a career as an artist, or as a stage or costume designer, or as a writer of plays and immensely diverting books, largely based on diaries of his experiences. He chose to devote himself almost exclusively to the theatre, however, and the Dublin Gate Theatre which he founded at the age of 28 with his enormously talented partner, Hilton Edwards, will stand as the most lasting monument to his memory.

There was a great need for a theatre like the Gate in the late 1920s. The Abbey Theatre was showing Irish drama to the world, and Edwards-Mac Liammóir felt that the time was ripe to show world theatre to Ireland. The venture they embarked upon brought freshness and excitement in plays hitherto unseen, in Edwards's directorial and lighting genius, in Mac Liammóir's settings, costumes and acting, in stylish and elegant presentations. A play-going public fed on a staple diet of healthy, but unvaried, bacon-and-cabbage could now sample the spicy delights of international cuisine. In its founding and in its survival through many years of fearful financial difficulties, the Gate pays ample tribute to the depth and doggedness of Mac Liammóir's practical commitment to Ireland.

In it, he acted more than three hundred roles, and many consider that his 'Hamlet' was the finest ever played by an Irish actor. In it, his own thirteen plays were performed, and all but one was a box-office success. The last, *Prelude in Kazbek Street*, has been described as the most sensitive and the most profound stage work written on the theme of the homosexual's dilemma in the area of meaningful human relationships. Foreign tours brought the Gate a measure of international recognition, but it was *The Importance of Being Oscar* which brought Mac Liammóir world-wide renown from 1960 onwards.

This solo recital, based on the life and writings of Oscar Wilde, raised the one-man show form of theatre to new heights. In devising it, writing linking material as brilliant in its content and wit as Wilde could have wished, and in giving it a performance of magic and artistry, he was acclaimed across four continents. And this pleased him not so much for reasons of personal vanity and reward as for the honour it reflected on Ireland through Wilde, an Irish writer, and through himself, an Irish actor.

In a tribute to his partner the evening he died, Hilton Edwards referred to this. 'Ireland has lost a great Irishman who loved his country in peace all his life, and served her in peace all his life, not without honour and distinction beyond her shores,' he said. 'This he was always careful to do, and this wish formed the basis of his work, in which he always tried to show Ireland as he wanted her to be.'

Since the death of Micheál Mac Liammóir there has been the expected deluge of clichés. An era has ended; his loss is irreparable, and so on. Clichés have the irritating habit of being invariably true. An era has, indeed, ended. His loss is, indeed, irreparable. Few men have done as much to reveal the beauty of the Irish language and promote its viability. Few have done as much to renew Irish theatre and bring to it elegance, quality and the severe disciplines demanded by the highest standards of professionalism. Few have done as much to encourage by word and example values of integrity and beauty in the arts. Few have done as much to practise the dying art of practical patriotism.

Ireland has not been ungenerous in acknowledging Micheál Mac Liammóir's dedication and contribution. He was elected a member of the Irish Academy of Letters; he was given the Lady Gregory Literary Award; he was, with his partner, made a Freeman of the City of Dublin; the country's two major universities conferred honorary doctorates on him; he was made an honorary life member of Irish Actors' Equity. In Denmark, the mayor of Elsinore presented him with the Kronborg Gold Medal after he played *Hamlet* in its historic location and France made him a Chevalier of the Legion d'Honeur.

Dr. Patrick Hillery, President of Ireland, the Taoiseach, Mr. Jack Lynch, several Cabinet-Ministers, Dr. Garrett FitzGerald, leader of the Opposition and leading representatives of every branch of art and culture attended his funeral. So did many hundreds of anonymous Irish whose lives he had enriched. If such a thing as adequate tribute can be paid to a person so gifted and so giving, it was paid.

VERY REV. DR. BRENDAN DEVLIN

professor of French at St. Patrick's College, Maynooth,
and writer in the Irish language

69

In the pages of his collection of essays *Ceo Meala Lá Seaca*, published in 1952, Micheál Mac Liammóir has left us his own graphic account of the meeting out of which was to come a theatre devoted entirely to plays in the Irish language, what was to become *Taibhdhearc na Gaillimhe*.

Travelling with Anew McMaster's company in the autumn and winter of 1927–28, Hilton Edwards and he had been endlessly planning for a theatre of their own, 'if only to stage *Diarmuid agus Gráinne*', which Mac Liammóir had recently completed and which, to his disappointment, had been refused by McMaster.

'While we were staying in Galway,' he recalls, 'our landlady came to say that there was a gentleman in the dining-room to see me. I went down, and found Liam O Briain. . . . We spent twenty minutes or so in conversation and then I burst out of the room to find Hilton.

' "Come down and meet Liam O Briain from the university," I said. "You and I are to found an Irish language theatre in Galway."

'I could hardly believe my ears. A theatre. A theatre in Ireland. And a theatre for the Irish language — no, it could not be true. A door opened in my mind and I saw a new and limitless world. I was in a way alone in this world; I had experience of the theatre and I knew Irish. . . . Maybe this was the chance to marry them. I was full of gratitude that day. I was drunk with enthusiasm.'

The following summer Edwards and Mac Liammóir left McMaster's company and returned to Galway for what was to be three years of heroic effort on Mac Liammóir's part as director, author, translator and actor. If at the end of that time the new venture of the Gate Theatre drew him back to Dublin, his burning vision of a triumphant Irish language theatre largely unfulfilled, it would be a mistake to think that his work for the Taibhdhearc was simply a failure. For one thing the Taibhdhearc still exists half a century later, much more adequately equipped than at its beginnings but still displaying the black curtain with its 'highly nationalist Celtic peacocks' painted for it by Mac Liammóir himself.

Much more importantly, of course, he created in the Taibhdhearc what can only be called a tradition, for there young actors and producers were trained in the Irish language to real artistic and theatrical standards. The founding of the Taibhdhearc accomplished that most difficult of achievements in such a revolutionary departure: it showed that it could be done, and done well. It is not only that many of the graduates of the Taibhdhearc went on to make their mark well beyond the limits of Galway, or of the Irish language, or of Ireland, but more importantly, a theatre was created in the Irish language which has endured; a theatre with its corpus of plays, original and translated, with actors and producers who have the example and the standards of their predecessors to inspire them to new efforts, and lastly a public which, small though it may be, assumes and expects the continued existence of a theatre in the Irish language, conditioned to the standards of art and not of some academic coterie.

The great occasion, of course, in the early days of the Taibhdhearc was the staging of Mac Liammóir's own romantic drama, *Diarmuid agus Gráinne*. It was something of a gala evening, the audience presided over by Mrs. Josephine MacNeill, as Mac Liammóir recalls, 'regal in a silver-white dress with her long strings of pearls and heavy golden-yellow hair'. In that first production the leads were played by Mac Liammóir himself and by Máire Ní Scolaí, with other names that were to be well known in support, Liam O Briain, Máirtín O Direáin, Proinsias Mac Diarmada. Clearly, in this play its author gave free rein to what was at one stage in his life a passionate inclination for 'the noble lady, Romanticism', as he says wryly in an essay written some twelve years later. And certainly *Diarmuid agus Gráinne* lives up to what its author expected of that same noble lady:

'Whatever side she casts those wonderful eyes of hers, she sees great seas deluged with light, and awful forests full of darkness and mystery. Her robes are the colour of flame, and the hawk-headed gods walk by her side, with enchanted rings upon their fingers. Her thoughts dwell with the gods and with the radiant and lovely creatures of her fancy, airy, nameless creatures that never were and never could be except in the hollowed places which their mistress treads with her shining feet.'

And yet, in that essay of 1940, Mac Liammóir admits that romantic theatre is a theatre of the past, making demands in acting and production which he now sees the Irish language theatre will not be able to meet for some time in the future. He might have added that it assumes a sensibility which appears increasingly a luxury in our ruthless times, and resources of expression which the Irish of the revival, not to speak of more fortunate languages, could hardly muster without affectation.

But of this the reader, or the theatre-goer, must judge for himself.

Costume design by Micheál Mac Liammóir for his *Diarmuid agus Gráinne*, 1928.

RICHARD PINE
concerts manager, Radio Telefís Eireann, author and lecturer

He was acclaimed a master of the harmony of line and colour in movement; that is one of his great secrets, and with each successive production his work has been more clearly recognised as an essential factor in, and an integral complement of, the enchanting inventions of the poets and musicians with whom he has worked. These words were written in 1913 by Arsène Alexandre about Léon Bakst, the most influential ballet and stage designer of the century, but they are also profoundly relevant to Micheál Mac Liammóir, since the influence of Bakst was central to his own work, and since the words summarise a major aspect of his theatrical achievement.

It is perhaps because I belong to a generation which did not see Micheál Mac Liammóir in his prime as an actor that I value him so much as an artist of another kind — as a stage designer and as an illustrator. Many patrons of the Gate Theatre will have taken for granted the regular programme credit: 'Setting and costumes designed by Micheál Mac Liammóir', particularly when the production featured him in a leading role. But his conception of the importance of the visual element in drama — combined with the choreographic skills of his partner Hilton Edwards — has contributed immensely to the development of the theatre both in Ireland and internationally, and his work as an illustrator of folk themes has earned him a permanent and significant place in the history of Irish art.

Micheál Mac Liammóir:
illustration for
Oidhcheanna Sidhe,
1922.

Micheál Mac Liammóir's work as a visual artist can, broadly speaking, be classified under three headings: his work for the theatre (designs for costumes and designs for stage settings); his illustrations for his own and others' books; and a series of pictures, mostly executed in his youth, and mostly illustrating scenes and themes from Celtic myth and legend, including sketches of close friends and the occasional — though, alas, rarely preserved — whimsical impression of a face or an abstract notion.

Many discoveries and several false starts, following the natural conclusion of his career as a child-actor, influenced the development of his graphic output. A period at the Slade was probably the least influential. 'The only talent I had was for ornament and decoration. I don't mean abstract design like William Morris wallpaper or a modern abstract, I mean decorative rather than representational. So the Slade was very little use to me in that practical way, except that I did learn to draw a man's or a woman's body with reasonable correctness, not with much individual style, but there wasn't scope for that.' (Conversation with R.P., 1976.) I am not sure that Hilton Edwards would agree with him, because as he has somewhat wryly observed 'his anatomy is frequently more expressive than correct.' (Introduction to exhibition catalogue, *Micheál Mac Liammóir, 'Designs and Illustrations, 1917–1972'*, Dublin, 1973.)

The most interesting survival from his adolescence is a copy of Pearse's

Micheál Mac Liammóir:
three illustrations for
An Mháthair by
Padraic Pearse, c. 1916.

An Mháthair agus sgéalta eile, given to him by his mother in 1916, in which he illustrated the blank page facing the opening of each story. His earliest published work—as far as can be discovered—were sketches of himself as Macduff's son in *Macbeth* in 1911 and as John in *Peter Pan* (1912) and a war-time cartoon 'The Damosel I left Behind Me' published in *Punch* in 1915. Inspired by the Gaelic League which he had joined in London in order to learn Irish, Micheál returned, following the Easter Week Rising, to Dublin, where he became known as an artist. Joseph Holloway encouraged him by buying his pictures. In 1917 Holloway recorded in his diary (*Joseph Holloway's Abbey Theatre*, edited by Hogan and O'Neill): 'Michael Willmore is a youth with real talent. . . . He has a fondness for Jack B. Yeats's work and produces some very clever imitations of his style in colour, but with a more refined line that emphasizes the crudeness of the method he mimics. Some of his black and white designs are really beautiful and clever, and all his work in whatever medium is full of imagination.' He was asked to illustrate stories published by the Talbot Press, such as T. H. Nally's *The Irish Santa Claus* and Séamus O'Kelly's *The Hillsiders*, and his own Irish stories, *Faery Nights* or *Oídhcheanna Sídhe*, published in 1922 with parallel English and Irish texts, in which the illustrations also appear both in English and Irish! Later he illustrated several volumes by Corkery and Pádraic O Conaire, including the latter's *Field and Fair*.

The influence of Arthur Rackham is evident in these pictures, as it is in what must be the only other surviving set of pictures from his 'teens, five 'Celtic Twilight' representations including 'Centaurs' (bearing a remarkable resemblance to Yeats, Beardsley, Shaw, George Moore and Casement) and another inspired by *Towards Democracy* by Edward

Carpenter, dated 1917. Titles such as 'Imeall an Domhain' (The Edge of the World), 'An Chéad Chuimhne' (The First Memory) and 'The Travelling Man' testify to his search for an Irish, national, identity, as do their various signatures, 'Miceal Willmore' and 'Miceal mac Uall-moir', for he had yet fully adopted his Irish name, which eventually became Micheál Mac Liammóir as it spelt.

He left Ireland again to travel with Máire O'Keeffe, a distant relative suffering from tuberculosis. A sketchbook survives from Davos, which he visited with Máire and her mother, Florence (Aunt Craven), in 1921–22. Although I had seen photographs of Micheál and Máire, and some stylised portraits of her, I had not realised until I recently saw these sketches that so many of his women's faces in his designs and illustrations are Máire's face. In designing costumes for specific actresses, of course, he would have in mind their particular characteristics — Coralie Car-michael, Meriel Moore and more recently Kate Flynn and Claire Mullen come most readily to mind — but often the face is a haunting memory of Máire's features, drawn and at the same time heightened by the tragic ambivalence of consumption. It is in Micheál's famous 'Madonna of the Roads' of 1927, for example, and in a portrait painted as a stage prop for the revival in 1969 of *Ill Met by Moonlight*.

The other major influences in what I think of as his pre-Gate career were those of Charles Ricketts and Aubrey Beardsley. As Hilton Edwards remarked in 1973, 'he himself would be the first to admit the fatality of an influence such as Beardsley's which, while teaching purity of line and the immeasurable value of space, by its very individuality thrusts those who are enthralled by it into servility.' The Beardsley influence, in the black and white, hermaphrodite, masked, self-abusive, yellow-nineties sense did not dominate Micheál's work for any length of time, unlike that of Harry Clarke or Yeats's friend W. H. Horton, and his relationship with it was a flirtation rather than a marriage or an illegitimacy. Nevertheless Beardsley taught him one thing which was

Micheál Mac Liammóir:
Design for Harlequin in
Nicolai Evreinov's
A Merry Death, 1929.

Micheál Mac Liammóir:
Design for Harlequin,
c. 1940.

not 'fatal' but has contributed to his own personal style: the 'servility' due to this *homme fatal* is more than outweighed by the legacy of the skill of draughtsmanship, this 'frightening definition of line', a definition of space by economic use of line and contrasts which, relieved and enlivened by Micheál's use of colour, distinguished theatre designs and established him as one of the foremost stage designers of his day, together with Bakst and Gordon Craig. His affinity with Craig is particularly noteworthy, considering the extent of their interests and achievements. Craig protested against 'the popularisation of Ugliness, the bearing of false witness against Beauty . . . the achievements of the Realistic Theatre . . . this anarchistic tendency.' Both Micheál and Hilton took a great deal, both in terms of courage and inspiration, from this man who, like themselves in many respects was far ahead of his time.

The main influence in Micheál's use of colour was Léon Bakst, whose costumes and settings he saw repeatedly at the Russian Ballet. His sense of the dramatic was heightened by the dancing of Nijinsky, Karsavina and Pavlova, the choreography of Fokine, Massine and Nijinsky himself, the music of Stravinsky and Ravel and the charisma of their impresario, Diaghilev. Bakst in a sense redeemed Micheál from his indebtedness to Beardsley and his imitators, and gave him the encouragement he needed to translate his feeling for immediate colour and line into dramatic movement. (Interviewed at the age of fifteen on the subject of the Russian Ballet he called it a 'jolly fine show'. This interviewer commented: 'His portfolio of drawings is full of impressions of Nijinsky, rough drafts of illustrations for Irish folk and fairy stories, and stray pencilled thoughts suggested by his wide reading.' *The Star*, 29 June 1915.)

One dominant motif inherited from the Nijinsky-Bakst ballets was that of Harlequin, which Micheál constantly drew and redrew. Of course in the case of *Full Moon for the Bride* (the designs were made in 1968) as well as *The Immortal Hour* (1944) and *The Speckledy Shawl* (1960), these exotic designs *were* intended for ballet, reconciled to the Celtic world of twilight, fairy and tragicomic heroism. But in general the drawings Micheál made during the fifty years of his career as a stage designer illustrate the application of a vivid imagination to the daily drudgery of mounting and realising productions — sometimes of classics, sometimes of acknowledged modern masterpieces, sometimes of experimental works by contemporary Irish and international playwrights.

Yeats's propaganda drew Micheál, like Synge, back to Ireland to partake of, and assist at, that 'terrible beauty' when he might have enjoyed a more extensive international career. His plans to become an artist having gone awry, and the death of Máire O'Keeffe having urged him to discover a new life force within himself, Hilton and his challenging ideas suddenly stimulated and galvanised him.

The beginning of the Edwards – Mac Liammóir partnership led to something greater than either of the two partners could individually have contributed. While the purpose of this essay is to survey Micheál's work as a visual artist, I must here salute the influence of Hilton Edwards, because, if Bakst had liberated Micheál from the domination of the Beardsley culture, Hilton's unadulterated enthusiasm for their new theatre harnessed him to a dynamo which gave his various disorganised ideas a single purpose. 'I was fascinated by the visual, and I

think that this was part of the thing that made Hilton and me want to make a theatre. . . . Ireland had never experienced the joy of the visible, as Italy has. Ireland is essentially an oral country: its greatest art, like that of England, is literature. . . . I wanted to add to that the visible side and the theatre was the obvious place to do it because I was a decorator, instinctively, and Hilton did a great deal of the visual too, because his sense of grouping and lighting and so on is visual, and I wanted to make scenery and dresses and make something beautiful to look at . . . *décor*, if you like, the French word covers the two sides.' (Conversation with R.P., 1976.)

Hilton's remarkable abilities as a producer/director, especially his skills in grouping and lighting, fertilised the ideas in Mac Liammóir's over-charged imagination and created a true partnership in which drama became as nearly as possible 'literature in movement' and 'dance' or 'ballet' took on a new meaning — particularly in the light of the amazingly small stage on which *Peer Gynt* and other triumphs were produced. The avowed intention of the Gate Theatre was to show the world to Ireland. Micheál's personal ambition was to awaken a consciousness of the visual in a country where it had had no previous stimulation — something which Yeats, Douglas Hyde and Lady Gregory had neglected in their predominantly *literary* revival. George Morrison has observed frequently that the Irish are a nation of 'ill-visualates', but if that failing has lessened in the past fifty years it is due, as far as the stage is concerned, primarily to Mac Liammóir, just as the major advance in stagecraft is due to the insight and cerebral honesty of Hilton Edwards. From the surviving evidence *Peer Gynt* and *The Old Lady Says 'No!'*, in particular, achieved this. In other early productions such as *Hamlet* or *Faust*, economy of design and of action appear to have hallmarked the productions. A static quality was achieved in the symbolism of *Salomé* which heightened the effect of the setting in which the ballet-like movement took place.

At this stage of the Gate's development the influence of Yeats's theories about the drama must still have been substantial (although the Gate's policies were different from, while complementary to, those of the Abbey). The static, symbolic nature of the Japanese Noh drama which appealed so strongly to Yeats also gave the Gate a new choreographic interest, particularly in connection with Yeats's own *The King of the Great Clock Tower*, staged in 1941. Micheál always attempted to absorb the oriental, exotic elements of his materials into the Celtic world which, with utter consistency for over sixty years, he was trying to realise for Irish people with a new meaning — away from blind nationalism, towards an understanding of a rediscovered past, a heritage which was valid as a passport to a virile future.

One of the most important of his Irish contemporaries was the Cubist painter Mainie Jellett who, with Evie Hone, was developing an art form which took its inspiration from Egypt, from Celtic art, from the *trecento*, and made live things of non-representational material. Mainie Jellett believed in a heroic period in art which had once more come alive, and like Yeats's poetic example I believe her work and ideas stimulated a lyrical and heroic quality in Micheál's early pictures: Eochaidh and Etáin, Diarmuid and Gráinne, Cuchulainn, Fionn Mac Cumhaill, the Children of Lir. Micheál's work was hardly ever abstract or non-representational but in his more symbolist pictures on Celtic or Persian themes and in some of his theatre designs—where, for example, action is minimised and dialogue almost takes on an extra dimension—I believe he did almost achieve a static quality just as Mainie Jellett achieved a rhythm in her geometric patterns. To emphasise this point I suggest that Mainie Jellett left ample evidence in her writings and in her art of her own deep concern for the interaction of form and colour, of pattern and rhythm, which must have affected both Micheál and Hilton and struck a common chord. In one sense it is disappointing that his commitments to the theatre prevented him from developing this: probably the high point, and his only really significant contributions to this field after the founding of the Gate, were his (rejected) designs for Covent Garden of *Tristan und Isolde* and his illustrations for *Scéalaíocht na Ríthe* by Tomás O Floínn and Proinsías Mac Cana (1956). This, like Colum's *Mogu of the Desert* (1931), had a strong Persian element in which the influence of Edmond Dulac and Kay Nielsen, (for example in their individual illustrations of *The Arabian Nights*) can be clearly seen. Micheál was unhappy about *Mogu*, both as a play and as a production, calling his designs 'false and unreal . . . nothing but half-hearted echoes . . . filtering down through Bakst and Edmond Dulac . . . nothing that came from myself' (*All for Hecuba*).

Similarly he came to regard his own *Diarmuid and Gráinne* as a failure, because it was written in the classical-revival framework of the nineteenth-century Celtic Twilight 'wallowing' which he abhorred, although I think the designs for both plays are very beautiful in their

Micheál Mac Liammóir :
Peasant sketch, c. 1928.

(left)
Micheál Mac Liammóir : Il Dottore.
Costume for *The Servant of Two Masters,* 1973.

(right)
Micheál Mac Liammóir : Pantalone.
Costume for *The Servant of Two Masters,* 1973.

own right. The nearest he came to Cubism on an international level
was in his illustrations of 1964 for his own prose poems *Blath agus
Taibhse* where I think we can find an expression, unique in all his
graphic work (outside the theatre), of an Irishness in the mainstream of
European art — at the same time primitive, elemental, sophisticated,
Celtic in the best sense of the word, and thoroughly continental. This is
perhaps best matched in his theatre designs by those for *Romeo and
Juliet.*

Micheál always maintained that Synge, alone among the Abbey
playwrights, had answered Yeats's call for a poetical drama. Micheál's
attempts in his own plays to bring deep-rooted Irish folklore onto the
contemporary stage should be mentioned here because their stagecraft
was completely involved with his visual concept. Referring to *Ill Met
By Moonlight* he said: 'As the twilight comes down, as light gets un-
certain, and things get distorted, or revealed in another way, they take
on another personality, a haystack becomes a giant, a tree becomes a
looming ghost, a far-off mountain seems glowing with flame. . . . I tried
a new trick, which is purely theatrical, of combining that world we've

(above left)
Micheál Mac Liammóir : Mrs. Cheveley, first dress.
(above right) Mabel Chiltern, first dress.
(below left) Mrs. Cheveley, second dress.
Costumes for *An Ideal Husband*, 1971.

been talking about, the world Yeats rediscovered, the mythological world which he shrouded in twilight, with a pleasant modern commonplace world — to marry those two worlds was my experiment.' (Conversation with R.P., 1976.)

These plays require not only an emotional response on the part of their audiences but also a cerebral commitment, what Keats called 'a willing suspension of disbelief', like most Symbolist drama. This does not mean, however, that Micheál's dramas are 'contrived'. It is interesting to note that Arsène Alexandre dealt with the same intellectual 'problem' in his essay on Bakst: 'the word "problem" implies a system to be worked out by argument. But to one who, like Bakst, *knows* how to clothe his figures . . . to him no reason is necessary — he sees, creates and accomplishes . . . his costumes seem to be the natural garment, the logical envelope, of the figures.' It is the same instinctive feeling for character and environment that hallmarks Micheál's own designs.

I think this is what Hilton had in mind when he said 'his work has, for me at least, a romantic beauty, an evocation of things other than the obvious and commonplace. An almost footlight glamour is never really absent from them, or at least *a light not seen by ordinary eyes*. Never is gaiety far from his work, and *there is always a sense of other-worldliness*, whether that other world be of the Sidhe or of those lands that lie

Micheál Mac Liammóir: *Tristan und Isolde*. Proposed design for Covent Garden.

behind the theatre curtain that is about to rise' (Catalogue introduction, 1973, my italics).

There is a currency and immediacy about Micheál's stage drawings, whether for sets or costumes — his costumes are filled by actors who are about to step towards the immediate audience, and while human figures seldom appear in his set designs they are always waiting in the wings beyond the confines of the paper on which the set has been drawn. Of all the recent designs which I have seen, the costumes for *The Taming of the Shrew* and *Servant of Two Masters* best illustrate the first point, and the sets for *Romeo and Juliet* and *The Drunkard* (the 1960 revival) the second. This vitality of what is not, after all, a finished canvas but working instructions for seamstresses and carpenters is achieved because the man who made them was an actor and a playwright, and a stage designer who is neither of these things cannot achieve the same vibrancy, however fertile his imagination may be.

One of the most fascinating and to me enigmatic facts is that while Micheál's own imagination was limited by the influences which shaped his early development, his work for the stage continued to be not merely relevant and appropriate to the production in hand but to complement the direction of his partner to such an extent that their presentations have been of a consistently high standard throughout these fifty years, and that the partnership has succeeded in frequently producing masterpieces in which the combination of author, play, players, designer and director and audience has placed them in the forefront of European drama. As evidence that the style which Micheál developed is not 'dated' I can cite the designs executed in 1972 for the Royal Shakespeare Company by Christopher Morley and Ann Curtis (featured in the 1973 exhibition of the Arts Council of Great Britain, 'Staging the Romans') which show the same enduring influence of Bakst and Gordon Craig, still vital and still valid, with a pedigree extending through Rembrandt to the oriental miniaturists.

Micheál
Mac Liammóir:
King Marke. Costume
for *Tristan und Isolde*
proposed for
Covent Garden.

Micheál insisted that 'my imagination stops dead at 1900'. This is somewhat misleading because, although he took little from his own generation, the Edwardian, he was not entirely out of sympathy with artistic developments at the turn of the century. Growing up after the European war he was entitled to think critically about his inherited culture. The major pioneers of the period owed their aesthetic origins to the 'Victorian' age. The iconoclastic Russian Ballet had its roots in romantic imperialism, sterile decadence, fertile symbolism, philistine capitalism, a polyglot society which could tolerate both Frith and Wilde, Ruskin and Whistler, Henry James and G. B. Shaw, which discovered Ibsen and at the same time idolised Bernhardt. And after all it was the society which lionised Micheál's first mentor, Sir Herbert Beerbohm Tree, the great actor-manager in whose tradition Micheál and Hilton both so obviously followed. Their ancestors, however disparate, were Pater, du Maurier, Baudelaire, William Morris, and Alfred Jarry, and they shared them with their contemporary cousins Cocteau, Brancusi, Picasso, Stravinsky, Joyce.

Micheál himself refashioned the heavy Victorianised Celtic ornament — long before he saw the true originals of the Book of Kells — and by lightening it without destroying its outline, conveyed a visual stimulus which he contributed to the creation of a modern theatre. He was a true pre-Raphaelite, relishing the hard line and deep primitive colours of Cimabue and Giotto, and he appreciated the fact that his contemporary, Picasso, was, consciously or unconsciously, reverting to that style. But he did not accept everything his contemporaries did, or unreservedly acclaim their achievements. 'I don't enjoy all these gentlemen's works, as I doubtless should,' he told me, talking of Stravinsky and Picasso and Joyce. 'I've already seen the blasts of winter — they were wintry artists, the heralds of the winter, which is to my mind what we're suffering from now. Winter rhymes with Pinter, doesn't it?'

As a judge of fashion he was scathing and contemptuous. Although he himself dressed colourfully and with — or to — effect, as if wearing one of his own designs, he appreciated the aesthetic merit of the conventional male evening wear, the severe, Beardsleyesque black and white setting off, perversely, the peacock splendour of the ladies' gowns, jewellery and *coiffure*. The mini-skirt he called 'an abomination — ladies who think they're Rosalind and look like a touring edition of Dick Whittington'. He took little interest in male fashions. Very few of his designs for male characters survive, apart from Shakespearean productions. When he was asked by *The Irish Times* what the well-dressed man would be wearing in 1974 he answered: 'Will there be any? There were none in 1973. . . . I should imagine that the keenest sartorial regret was felt among members of our sex at the beginning of the nineteenth century when the knee breeches, and the flared and waisted coats and the brilliant colours of the previous century were giving way to the tubular trousers, and the more sombre frock or cut-away coats of what was then the new age.' It must have been a source of great regret to Micheál that he could not in his later years design more eighteenth-century costumes. Perhaps this explains the vigorous designs for the men in *The Servant of Two Masters*.

He was equally dismissive of modern art and architecture. Contemporary works in general appalled him. He treasured skill and craftsmanship and found them lacking. Having learnt from the finest masters in both acting and designing he was disgusted by the insincerity, carelessness and lack of insight or preparation which he saw all around him — what Craig called 'this false-witnessing Realism, this traitor to the Imagination — this idolatry of ugliness'. I think he probably took great solace in Craig's words, written in 1912: 'It has never been the purpose of art to make uglier the ugliness of things, but to transform and make the already beautiful more beautiful, and, in following this purpose, art shields us with sweet influences from the dark sorrows of our weakness.' If at the end of his life he turned his face to the wall and began to look more searchingly into the past it was because he found nothing new to stimulate or challenge him. It was not a question of honesty: 'Honesty doesn't interest me, effect does.' He did not believe that death was the end: he believed in reincarnation, he knew he had lived in an age before 'Realism' and perspective had become necessary in art, when bold line and colour and dancing movement had been enough to achieve supreme effect.

HILTON EDWARDS

actor, director and co-founder of the Dublin Gate Theatre

Peter Luke, whom I have known ever since he was a small boy and who, by the time he had grown a grey beard, had become a member of the Gate Board of Directors, has asked me to write something brief about my partner — my late partner, Micheál Mac Liammóir. Brief! Oh, 'would I were an Aubrey'!

For fifty-one years Micheál and I have been partners and at the end of that time our minds were entwined, our thoughts barely needing to be expressed in words. Of course many sparks flew between us. Sometimes he was the anvil and I the hammer, sometimes the positions were reversed. But the sparks that flew conflagrated into a small blaze that became two entities: our lasting friendship and the Dublin Gate Theatre.

Elsewhere the history of the Gate has been written, and doubtless will be again. It is not my purpose to reveal or analyse any of this; just to tell what I have learned of him from his own lips.

Born Alfred Willmore in Ireland, of a father whose mother was Spanish, he spent his kindergarten years in Cork, at a nuns' school. His father, a corn merchant, shifted with his whole family, his wife, his five children, Dorothy, Christine, Peg, Marjorie and the youngest, his son Alfred, to London where they settled in varying conditions of happiness and, I fear, not on the father's part with any great success. He, as Micheál often said, was a colour-blind but brilliant draughtsman, an artist manqué and, therefore, not a very successful businessman. So Micheál's early years were a period of near poverty which in later life made him careful of farthings, but his generosity of spirit made him lavish even to his enemies in their need.

Micheál, a pretty, curly-headed boy at eight years old, was an obvious butt for the toughs in the council school in which he found himself, and this I think left on him a small but lasting scar. 'Get out on the field and kick the ball,' yelled the master in a markedly Cockney accent. Young Micheál does so — through his own goal — and got 'the bird' for the first and only time.

As has been written elsewhere Micheál acted from the first before his mother's bedroom mirror, and later on the stage of his Majesty's Theatre before the great Sir Herbert Beerbohm Tree. In this, his first public performance, he was soon promoted to the hero, 'King Goldfish', where he was opposed by the villain 'little Noël Coward', his junior by a month or so. This was soon followed by an invitation by Tree to play in *Macbeth*, later in the name part of *Oliver Twist* to Tree's Fagin, later still as Benjamin in *Joseph and His Brethren*, and so on through a quite triumphant career. All this time he was being tutored by his most loved sister Marjorie — later to become Mrs. Anew McMaster.

At this stage Micheál was obviously much fêted and even a little spoiled. Later, however, his voice broke and he found himself no longer a boy and not yet a man. So to the Slade School of Art (the youngest pupil ever taken), where he met, by some strange fate, a distant cousin (how remote I have never been sure), Máire O'Keeffe. There was nothing amatory in the relationship which developed but it was none-the-less very strong and binding and they opened up together an inner and almost secret life which never ceased until Máire's tragically early death.

Micheál made it clear to me when, in later life, he had such a success with his *Oscar*, that Wilde had never been an influence on him. An enormous interest yes, an evocation of tragedy and, of course, often of laughter and admiration, but the supreme influence on his life, he insists, was W. B. Yeats. This, his true influence, enwrapped both his cousin Máire and himself and resulted in their coming with Máire's mother, Mrs. O'Keeffe, to live in Ireland. Mrs. O'Keeffe, whom I remember well, an endearing and charming old lady she appeared to me then, always craving something — 'Oh! I do crave a new stove' — which in turn caused her to be called 'Craven', a name by which she became known ever after, even signing her letters 'Craven'.

Trouble soon followed. In Howth Máire was found to have developed tuberculosis in its most virulent form. In those pre-penicillin days there was but one course: by hook or by crook between Craven's meagre allowance and Micheál's still somewhat meagre earnings with his pen — both writing and drawing — they travelled to Davos in Switzerland where for five years he lived with them, helping in their support.

Micheál's talents: there were so many that even in his long life of 78 years, none of them was quite developed to the full: there just was not time. His early influence was Beardsley and, as I venture to think without much knowledge, Arthur Rackham, Bakst and Cocteau, though he soon developed a strength of line and individuality of style which were all Mac Liammóir.

Tragedy followed: Máire, seemingly cured, they returned to Ireland. Later, the three of them, Máire, Craven and Micheál, revisited the south of France on holiday. There Máire died. Micheál, desolate, dispirited, almost lost, fled to the protection of his early mentor, his sister Marjorie, now married to the Shakespearean actor, Anew McMaster. Here, in his half-remembered technique of acting and a rapidly increasing skill in scenic decoration, he found some refuge. And this is where I enter the story.

Egotist as I fear I am, I have little recollection of my early childhood. Fond parents and a comfortable home, money seemed plentiful until the coming of World War I when everything started to go. I was the only child of my father's second marriage: his first wife had died. My father's death was followed by my mother's and then her sister's, so that I found myself the last of my line with no blood relation that I knew of in the world. I had studied music with my mother but either her not-too-thorough technique or my waywardness had given me not more than a rudimentary knowledge so that later, when I had the opportunity of studying under a great master, and even gained some facility with theory and orchestration, I found myself still musically able to run and leap, but not to walk. In fact I am a bit of a musical fake, but it has served my purpose. I did, however, have a baritone voice of some power which I managed to get trained, though my coming to Ireland stopped the training before my voice had reached maturity, but I am anticipating.

With the death of my father our family fortunes were at a very low ebb and, after numerous vicissitudes, I found myself — I hardly know how — spouting speeches of Cyrano de Bergerac before the famous figure of Mr. Robert Atkins, director of the Old Vic in the time of Lilian Bayliss.

'No experience,' barked Atkins. 'Go and get some.'

'How?' asked I.

Answer came in Atkins's drawl. 'Charles Doran is taking a company on tour. Say I sent you.'

That afternoon Charles Doran engaged me at the sum of £3 per week to play the First Player in *Hamlet* and to assistant stage manage (little did I know in those days what this entailed, a very different picture from today) and a multitude of other parts, sometimes as much as five programmes in a repertory of plays of Shakespeare.

In this company I toured for a year. Donald Wolfit was the other assistant stage manager and my senior. The stage manager used to call 'worms' and we used to wriggle up. After a few weeks Ralph (now Sir Ralph) Richardson joined the company, also his first job. At the end of this year we had visited Belfast, Dublin and finally Cork Opera House, the bill for which still hangs upon my wall. From there, back to the Old Vic where Atkins this time engaged me. The Old Vic was just steaming up to its tercentenary celebrations and was doing all the Shakespeare plays so that they might be said to have completed the canon by that date. So one way and another, I have played in every Shakespeare play except *King John* and *All's Well*. How nice, though, it would be to be able to say that I had played in the whole canon.

My last job in London was in the now bombed Royalty Theatre, in the Jewish play, *The Dybbuk*. (Incidentally, I am not Jewish. If I were I should proudly proclaim it.) In the cast of *The Dybbuk* was Peter Godfrey who had started the original Gate Theatre in London. *The Dybbuk* came to an end and I was informed that an actor called Anew McMaster was looking for a young actor to take the place of someone who was unable to fulfil his contract to play Iago, the King in *Hamlet*, MacDuff and several other roles. I had a little time out, my mother was dead and I had nothing to keep me in London. For five weeks . . . why not? I came to Ireland.

On the steps of the Town Hall in Enniscorthy, Co. Wexford, I came face to face with Micheál Mac Liammóir. Now, what can I say for the next fifty-one years? I open in my imagination a prop basket and in it see protruding the props of six hundred plays.

Micheál was immediately friendly to me and helped me to learn my multitudinous lines; he was bereaved of his cousin; I lately bereft of my mother. This seemed in some curious way to be a link between us and our friendship soon became affection. We tired the sun with talking. We tramped the lanes of Enniscorthy and many another country lane, discussing theatre. Ideas poured from us. Micheál with his actor's training and his Tree influence tended always towards the pictorial and the decoratively representational. I — lately under the influence of Appia, the impractical Gordon Craig and the like — was having my eye stretched in a contrary direction while at the same time being lured by Micheál's fascinating pictorialism. I think it was this pull, the conflict if you like, which, battered out on the anvil of our minds, occasionally blazed into some of our best work. Eventually it became difficult to know where Micheál stopped and I started.

Micheál was considered the artist, I the tough business man, and yet it was Micheál who had the common sense, the down-to-earth quality which I so sadly lack, combined with a toughness as immovable as a rock. Even 'Craven' would say 'You can't change Micky.' But, out of this seething cauldron, things began to grow.

Micheál had written his first play *Diarmaid agus Gráinne*, which was produced and directed by himself at the start of 'An Taibhdhearc na Gaillimhe', The Irish Language Theatre in Galway. At this I assisted in a very minor — though most interested — way. Micheál had translated the play into English. McMaster wanted to put on the English version but he professed himself too tired to do it. Micheál in despair asked me if I would like to produce it. In agreeing that I would, I unconsciously lit a bomb. The play never went on with the McMaster Company and I swore that I would put on the play in Dublin within the year if I had to build a theatre to do it.

Now, there is seldom only one reason why anything is done and I think the Gate Theatre came into being for many reasons, among them that:

> Micheál and I wanted to stay together — a thing not very easy in the professional theatre.
>
> I had sworn to put on his play.
>
> We were both full of ideas for putting on plays new to Dublin. This was particularly dear to Micheál's heart, as he wished Dublin to have all the appurtenances of a capital city and not to be considered a province of any other country—plays from the Continent, plays from the outside world. This also presented a limitation because they were nearly all translations which are notoriously less good than the originals.
>
> Ignobly, I wanted certain parts which no one else would let me play, and so did Micheál.

Well, with the help of Madame D. Bannard Cogley (Toto) her friend, Gearóid O'Lochlainn, her son, Mitchel, and the use of a little cabaret they were running in South William Street, we planned and, upon the borrowed resources of £15 from Mrs. O'Keeffe, we decided to take the Peacock Theatre for a limited period. Lennox Robinson was heard to say 'Ah! They won't last a fortnight' and this did much to activate my stubborn nature.

Well, the Peacock was too small to do anything, so we decided that we might as well do everything. We opened with *Peer Gynt* and it was voted a success.

After two seasons in which we made nothing, and lived on nothing but the kindness of friends, we had created something of a little reputation — much helped by Con Curran of *The New Statesman*—a grateful tribute to whom I have written elsewhere. Living in what was then Groome's Hotel, we one day spied the present Gate Theatre. Micheál's book *All For Hecuba* describes the rest of this story.

Almost the first thing I was aware of in Micheál was his strange musical gift. He played the piano brilliantly, but knew no note of music. I was enough of a musician to be able to read a score and I have sat with the score on my knee and watched Micheál go through a most fascinating series of modulations to keep himself in the keys he knew.

Musically he was playing what the composer had written though in the most fantastically different keys. I asked him how he did it and he replied 'I do not know, but, if I see a keyboard and two shadowy hands playing on it, I know I can do it, and if I do not, I cannot.'

Micheál's languages: I used to say he had all the talents of a good *maître d'hôtel*. His English, to my ear beautiful but definitely Irish-accented, was mellifluous and pure. His French was equally good and, for him, the language of social contact. In Spanish, his language of passion, he was equally fluent. If he tripped on a rug, it was in Spanish he swore. In German and Italian he was fluent though, I believe, insecure. But it was Irish that was the language of his heart. In it all his diaries were written and all his stage directions on his acting scripts, leaving somewhat of a problem for his unfortunate understudy.

Now, I see Micheál as Hamlet. They say nobody is altogether bad or altogether good in *Hamlet*. I did not want him to take it to London because Gielgud had just swept the boards with his performance, but I did not have the heart to stop him. The time was not advantageous, though Sir Compton McKenzie said that Micheál and Barrymore are the two best Hamlets of his remembrance.

To me, Micheál's creation of The Speaker in Denis Johnston's *The Old Lady Says No!* will always be incomparable. Denis had called it 'A Symphony in Green' and then had crossed this out on the manuscript. I saw it, not as a symphony, but as a concerto with a solo instrument and Micheál played it as such, running the whole gamut of Irishry with a rhythmical sense which equalled my musical vision. He created a never-to-be-forgotten character, redolent of comedy, tragedy, and biting irony, all of which were inherent in what I still regard as Denis's finest and most prophetic play.

When I think of Robert Emmet's meeting with the statue of Grattan, like Oedipus before the Sphinx, and Grattan's speech, which begins:

'Ah, the love of Death creeping like a mist at the heels of my countrymen. . . .'

This speech alone makes *The Old Lady Says No!* as vital now as when it was written.

Again, glancing in the basket, I see the ragged jacket of Heathcliffe in *Wuthering Heights*. In this latter part Micheál gave a performance of such penetration that I am still hypnotised by its memory.

Then again in *Berkeley Square*, Micheál appearing out of the window of the present to the past and saying: 'I knew it would look like this.' But there are so many parts it is impossible to consider even a tithe of them. One must not forget his outrageous sense of comedy—his Carmen Miranda, his Madame Relâche in his own *Home for Christmas*; his lively sketches with Jimmy O'Dea, his ebullient comedy sense which was not far from him either off stage or on, because even in Micheál's most serious moments there was this lightness of touch, this twinkle in the eye. Whereas he was capable of unshakable intolerance at times, perhaps his greatest capacity of all, either on or off the stage, was his alchemic sense of revealing. In reading a book, or strolling along the street, he could reveal a beauty which would otherwise remain unseen. But he had the double qualities of the revealer, and revealed qualities in others which they did not know about.

Towards the end of his life his eyesight had become stricken. On one occasion while filming he was not warned about the danger of looking into powerful camera lights. This brought on cataracts and eventually caused almost total blindness. With the realisation that, for this reason only, his acting career was drawing to a close, there came a terrible depression over him. To Micheál now was revealed a black side of life instead of the glories which had been previously so readily visible to him.

Meanwhile he had devised a one-man show, *The Importance of Being Oscar.* Never will his friends forget the first night at the Gaiety Theatre, then the Apollo, The Royal Court, The Haymarket and in America: New York, Broadway, and in South America and South Africa . . . Australia. Triumph followed him everywhere and this he followed by his other two shows, *I Must be Talking to My Friends* and *Talking About Yeats.*

There are so many things I could write about, but I must curtail myself. Our early days at the Gate when we transferred to the Rotunda would never have been possible without the assistance of Lord Longford until an unhappy divergence, based on an offer we had received to visit the Royal Opera House in Cairo, split our Companies. After this we subsisted on our various tours until we discovered we were pouring the profits of Micheál's one-man-show successes, as well as my more meagre film and other extramural activities, into the Gate to keep it alive.

Realising that this could not go on, and that a time would come when age alone would demand some savings, I tried to put a stop to it and only through the good offices of Terence de Vere White, Charles Haughey and others was the Gate put into a position to continue. We were then able to devote a little of our savings towards a rapidly approaching old age, though we had not allowed for inflation and the drop in the pound.

Always Micheál's problem was the fear of age — the heritage of the child actor. This he fought by all sorts of artificial means which deceived nobody, not even himself, and probably the noblest moment of all was when he, already stricken by a fall, awaited an operation on his head. Holding my hand — after a moment's hesitation — he nodded to his nurses to shave him to the skull, exposing a brow as magnificent as that, one likes to think, of Socrates. At that moment I felt the man's true strength and his most wise insight into life and even, perhaps, death.

This all too sketchy and incomplete impression of my partner will, of course, be considered partial. It is partial and to say otherwise would be a thumping lie. Of course I am partial — you see I admired and loved the man. I cannot hope to replace him. I can only hope that enough of his greatness has rubbed off on me to enable me to continue the work we have started for whatever time is left to me.

Hilton Edwards. Photograph by Harsch, Dublin.

Micheál Mac Liammóir
in *The King of the Great
Clock Tower* by
W. B. Yeats, 1942.

Micheál Mac Liammóir
and Betty Chancellor in
*A Midsummer Night's
Dream*, 1933.

COLM O BRIAIN
director of An Chomhairle Ealaíon/The Arts Council

TOWARDS THE FUTURE

A partnership of all the talents! How else can one describe a half century of brilliant personal achievements and a major influence in the shaping of modern theatre in Ireland? The unique individual contributions of Micheál Mac Liammóir and Hilton Edwards when combined created the driving force of Irish theatre, opening new horizons on the international repertoire and giving new life to the classics. This is the inheritance of the first fifty years; the second fifty must be founded on that inheritance.

In trying to see what lies ahead for the Gate the questions of tradition and succession have to be considered. It is a common Irish failing to seek refuge from the present in imaginary traditions, and where traditions do exist to use them as a defence against new perspectives and developments. Strong individualism, so essential for creative excellence, is generally unthinking of the future or sceptical about being able to influence it. Valuable traditions can be established and handed down only when there is an opportunity to take a long-term view. In the field of the arts the challenges and the obstacles of the present leave little energy or time for planning the future.

The support from the State, which the Gate Theatre now receives, came late in the day — after forty years of unacknowledged hard work and battling against seemingly impossible odds. The genius of Hilton Edwards and Micheál Mac Liammóir flourished in spite of the educational and financial restrictions of the time. These restrictions made it virtually impossible to train, to develop, to hand on the unique perspective and skills which these two men brought to the theatre.

If at this point Micheál Mac Liammóir and Hilton Edwards were to begin again, they might not choose to envelop themselves in any tradition which could suffocate their talent. They would have confidence, taking inspiration from the past, in their own abilities to create new excitement on the stage and to break their own new ground. The truth is that Micheál Mac Liammóir and Hilton Edwards are irreplaceable. Between them they excelled in six roles — actor, director, writer, administrator, set and costume designer, lighting designer. It is a reflection on the Irish theatre in the 'seventies that one might find two or three people to fill two or three of these functions reasonably well. It would be difficult to find six people to do each function as well; impossible to find two capable of all between them.

The direction which the Gate will take during the second half of its first century may be very different from anything that I have been able to imagine. It is not possible to plan for the happy chance that brings the exceptional talent along just at the right time. At this point in the theatre's history, however, it is difficult to imagine that the achievement of the past fifty years can be matched. The initiative still rests with the Gate itself. When it decides to explore the future, the support and energies of the Arts Council will be available to help in the task.

Micheál Mac Liammóir in *It's Later Than You Think*, 1971. Photo : Fergus Bourke.

Hilton Edwards in
Cyrano de Bergerac,
1932.

Micheál Mac Liammóir
in *Tolka Row*, 1951.

PRODUCTIONS 1928-1978
presented by
Edwards – Mac Liammóir Dublin Gate Theatre Productions Limited
Compiled by Patricia Turner

First Season, 1928–1929
at the Peacock Theatre

> *The company, under the title of the Dublin Gate Theatre Studio, opened at the Peacock Theatre, which they had leased from The National Theatre Society, on 14 October 1928.*

October 1928
Peer Gynt by Henrik Ibsen
Revived in 1932 and 1940.
The Hairy Ape by Eugene O'Neill

November
Diarmuid agus Grainne by Micheál Mac Liammóir
First production in English. Revived in 1930.

December
Salome by Oscar Wilde
First production in the British Isles.
The Theatre of the Soul by Nickolas Evreinov

January 1929
Six Stokers who own the Bloomin' Earth by Elmer Greensfelder
Anna Christie by Eugene O'Neill
Revived in March 1929, 1943 and 1953.

Second Season, 1929
at the Peacock Theatre

February
The Power of Darkness by Leo Tolstoy

March
Juggernaut by David Sears
Revived in 1930.

April
The Adding Machine by Elmer Rice

May
R.U.R. by Karel Capek
Revived in 1931.
The Unknown Warrior by Paul Raynal

June
Tristram & Iseult by An Philbin
First Production.
The Little Man by John Galsworthy
A Merry Death by Nickolas Evreinov
The Old Lady Says 'No' by E. W. Tocher (Denis Johnston)
First Production. Revived in 1931, 1934, 1935, 1941, 1947 and 1948.

September
The Ford of the Hurdles by Micheál Mac Liammóir (at the Mansion House)
First Production. Revived at the Gate Theatre in 1933.

Third Season, 1930
at the Gate Theatre

> *The company, now called the Dublin Gate Theatre Company Limited opened its third season on 17 February 1930 in the Assembly Rooms, Rotunda Buildings. These premises re-named the Gate Theatre have remained as the home of the Edwards – Mac Liammóir company to the present day.*

February
Faust by Johann Wolfgang von Goethe

March
Berkeley Square by Balderston and Squire
Revived in 1932, 1936 and 1940.

April
Wife to a Famous Man by Martinez Sierra
The Terrible Meek by Rann Kennedy
Gas by Georg Kaiser
Easter 1916 by Micheál Mac Liammóir
First Production. Revived in 1932.

May 1929	**Simoom** by August Strindberg
	Ten Nights in a Bar Room adapted from Pratt by Peter Godfrey
	The Witch by Wiers Janssen
June	**The Light Comedian** by Herman Ould

Fourth Season, 1930–1931
at the Gate Theatre

August 1930	**The Beaux' Stratagem** by George Farquhar
	First Irish Production for one hundred years.
September	**Tiger Cats** by Karen Bramsen
	The Hunger Demon (The Son of Learning) by Austin Clarke
	First Irish Production.
October	**Back to Methuselah** by Bernard Shaw
	Presented as a three-night cycle.
November	**A Flutter of Wings** by T. C. Murray
December	**The Merchant of Venice** by William Shakespeare
	Revived in 1956 and 1977.
	The Lady of Belmont by St John Irvine
	A sequel to The Merchant of Venice
	Christmas Pie. An International Variety Entertainment. This included
	The Fourth Wise Man by An Philbin
	Princely Fortune adapted from Su Ting Po by Kwei Chen
	Little Sister adapted from Su Ting Po by Kwei Chen
	The Devil Comes to Alcatraz by W. H. Fulham
	The Nativity, adapted by Lady Gregory from Douglas Hyde
January 1931	**Bride** by Ulick Burke
	First Production.
February	**Sweeney Todd**
March	**Tsar Paul** by Dimitri Merejkowski
	Revived in 1931 and 1943.
	Dublin Revue. A Variety Entertainment by E. W. Tocher (Denis Johnston), Frank O'Connor, Tom Purefoy, etc.
April	**The Man with a Load of Mischief** by Ashley Dukes
	Where the Cross is Made by Eugene O'Neill
	The Mollusc by H. H. Davies

Fifth Season, 1931–1932
at the Gate Theatre

August 1931	**Lady Windermere's Fan** by Oscar Wilde
	Revived in 1973.
	The Government Inspector by Nikolai Gogol
September	**The Melians** by the Earl of Longford
October	**Jew Suss** by Lionel Feuchtwanger, adapted by Ashley Dukes
	The Dead Ride Fast by David Sears
	First Production.
	The Archdupe by Percy Robinson
November	**Youth's the Season—?** by Mary Manning
	First Production.
December	**Mogu of the Desert** by Padraic Colum
	First Production.
February 1932	**Death Takes a Holiday** by Alberto Cassella, adapted by Walter Ferris
	Revived in 1933, 1937 and 1940.
	Hamlet by William Shakespeare
	Revived in 1934, 1935, 1937, 1940, 1941, 1952 and 1957.
	Topaze by Marcel Pagnol
March	**Obsession in India** by Richard E. Goddard
	First Production.
	Queens and Emperors by the Countess of Longford
	First Production.
	The Singer by Padraic Pearse
	The Man Who Married a Dumb Wife by Anatole France
	Carmilla, adapted by the Earl of Longford from J. Sheridan le Fanu
	First Production. Revived in 1933 and 1937. Egyptian tour 1937.

Sixth Season, 1932–1933
at the Gate Theatre

August 1932	**The Cherry Orchard** by Anton Chekov
	The Way of the World by William Congreve
September	**Therese Raquin**, adapted from Emile Zola
	Dark Waters by Dorothy Macardle
	First Production.
October	**An Ideal Husband** by Oscar Wilde
	Revived in 1945 and 1972, when it ran for nineteen weeks.
November	**Romeo and Juliet** by William Shakespeare
	Revived in 1936 and 1971.
	The Seagull by Anton Chekov
December	**Cyrano de Bergerac** by Edmond Rostand
	Don Juan by James Elroy Flecker
February 1933	**Agamemnon** by Aischylos, translated by the Earl and Countess of Longford
	The whole of the Oresteian trilogy was played under this title.
	Storm Over Wicklow by Mary Manning
	First Production.
	Saint Patrick's Day by Richard Brinsley Sheridan
	Mr. Jiggins of Jigginstown by the Countess of Longford
	First Production.
May	**A Bride for the Unicorn** by E. W. Tocher (Denis Johnston)
	First Production. Revived in 1935.
June	**Crime at Blossoms** by Mordaunt Sharp

Seventh Season, 1933–1934
at the Gate Theatre

September 1933	**Grania of the Ships** by David Sears
	First Production.
	Yahoo by the Earl of Longford
	Revived in 1935 and in the London Season 1935.
October	**The Importance of Being Earnest** by Oscar Wilde
	Revived in 1935, 1936, 1938 and 1971. Egyptian tour 1937.
November	**Richard III** by William Shakespeare
	Blood and Sand by V. Blasco Ibanez
December	**A Midsummer Night's Dream** by William Shakespeare
	Revived in 1940.
January 1934	**Wuthering Heights**, adapted by Ria Mooney and Donald Stauffer from Emily Brontë
	Revived in 1935, 1939, 1940 and 1944.
	Storm Song by E. W. Tocher (Denis Johnston)
	First Production.
February	**Liliom** by Frantz Molnar
	The Dark Lady of the Sonnets by Bernard Shaw
	The New Girl by the Countess of Longford
	Before Breakfast by Eugene O'Neill
	Apollo in Mourne by Richard Rowley
April	**Children in Uniform** by Christa Winsloe
	Happy Family by Mary Manning
	First Production.

Eighth Season, 1934–1935
at the Gate Theatre

October 1934	**Julius Caesar** by William Shakespeare
	Revived in 1936 and 1957. Egyptian tour 1936.
November	**The Provok'd Wife** by John Vanburgh
December	**The Drunkard** by William Smith of Boston
	Revived in 1941, 1948, 1949 and 1960.
January 1935	**Lady Precious Stream** by S. I. Hsiung
	Squaring the Circle by Valentin Kataev
	Ascendancy by the Earl of Longford

February 1935	**Three Leopards** by Cecil Monson
	First Production.
March	**Magic** by G. K. Chesterton
	Othello by William Shakespeare
	Revived 1945, 1953 and 1961. Egyptian tour 1937.
June 1935	London Season: **Yahoo, Hamlet** and **The Old Lady Says 'No'.**

Ninth Season, 1935–1936
at the Gate Theatre

October 1935	**The Marriage of Saint Francis** by Henri Gheon
	The Taming of the Shrew by William Shakespeare
	Revived in 1972. Egyptian tour 1936.
November	**Crime and Punishment,** adapted from Dostoievsky
December	**Not for Children** by Elmer Rice
	Revived in 1954.
January 1936	**Payment Deferred** by Jeffrey Dell
March–April	First Tour to Cairo and Alexandria: **Berkeley Square, Romeo and Juliet, Payment Deferred, Hamlet, The Taming of the Shrew, Heartbreak House** and **The Provok'd Wife.**

Tenth Season, 1936–1937
at the Gate Theatre

Independent Management of Hilton Edwards and Micheál Mac Liammóir as Dublin Gate Theatre Productions.

July 1936	**Master of the Revels** by Don Maquis
	First Production.
August	**When Lovely Woman** by Lennox Robinson
	First Production.
September	**Close Quarters** by W. O. Somin
	Egyptian tour 1937.
	The Marvellous History of Saint Bernard by Henri Gheon
	Portrait in Marble by Hazel Ellis
	Egyptian tour 1937.
October	**Victoria Regina** by Laurence Houseman
November	**Twelfth Night** by William Shakespeare
	Laburnum Grove by J. B. Priestley
December	**Brand** by Henrik Ibsen
	The School for Scandal by Richard Brinsley Sheridan
	Revived in 1943. Egyptian tour 1937.
February–March 1937	Second tour to Cairo and Alexandria: **Othello, Death Takes a Holiday, Portrait in Marble, Twelfth Night, The School for Scandal, Close Quarters, Carmilla, The Importance of Being Earnest** and **Laburnum Grove.**

Eleventh Season, 1937–1938
at the Gate Theatre

August 1937	**The Infernal Machine** by Jean Cocteau
	Night Must Fall by Emlyn Williams
	Revived in 1938, 1939, 1940 and 1943.
September	**Victoria (The Golden Sovereign)** by Laurence Houseman
October	**Macbeth** by William Shakespeare
	Revived in 1939.
November	**Judgement Day** by Elmer Rice
	Richard of Bordeaux by Gordon Daviot
	Murder like Charity by Andrew Ganly
	Seasons in Cork, Belfast and Cardiff followed. The Company went on tour to Cairo, Alexandria, Malta and Athens in 1938.

Twelfth Season, 1938–1939
at the Gate Theatre

August 1938	**The Comedy of Errors** by William Shakespeare
	Don Juan in Hell by Bernard Shaw
	Revived in 1943 and 1973.
	Hollywood Pirate, adapted from Marcel Archard's **Le Corsaire** by Micheál Mac Liammóir
September	**Unguarded Hour**, adapted from Otto Bastien
	Juliet in the Rain by Lenormand's **'Les Rates:** Translated and adapted by Micheál Mac Liammóir
October	**Mourning Becomes Electra** by Eugene O'Neill
	Revived in 1942.
November	**Women Without Men** by Hazel Ellis
December	**And So to Bed . . .** by J. B. Fagan

Seasons in Cork, Belfast, Ljubljana, Zagreb, Belgrade, Salonika, Sofia and Bucharest followed in 1939. Plays presented were: **The Comedy of Errors, Don Juan in Hell, Night Must Fall, Unguarded Hour, The Importance of Being Earnest, And So to Bed . . . , Wuthering Heights** and **Death Takes a Holiday.**

Thirteenth Season, 1939–1940
at the Gate Theatre

August 1939	**Will Shakespeare** by Clemence Dane
September	**I Have Been Here Before** by J. B. Priestley
	Pygmalion by Bernard Shaw
	Revived in 1946.
October	**Marrowbone Lane** by Robert Collis
	First Production. Revived in 1941.
November	**Third Party Risk** by Lenox and Ashley
	The Ascent of F6 by W. H. Auden and Christopher Isherwood
	A Hundred Years Old by the Brothers Quintero
	Revived 1945. CEMA *tour 1945.*
December	**The Merry Wives of Windsor** by William Shakespeare

At this time the regular seasons ended and the Company played several seasons annually in the Gaiety and the Gate theatres, with a break in continuity from late 1947 to Autumn 1948. The Gate and Gaiety seasons were then resumed and continued until the late 1950's.

At the Gaiety Theatre

February 1940	**Where Stars Walk** by Micheál Mac Liammóir
	First Production. Revived 1942, 1945 and 1952.
March	**Gaslight** by Patrick Hamilton
	The Dreaming Dust by Denis Johnston
	First Production. Revived in 1955.
September	**The Masque of Kings** by Maxwell Anderson
October	**Rebecca** by Daphne du Maurier
November	**No Traveller Returns** by Bertha Selous

At the Gate Theatre

November	**Roly-Poly**, adapted from de Maupassant by Lennox Robinson
	First Production. Withdrawn after three performances at the request of the Minister for Justice.
December	**Granite** by Clemence Dane
	Snapdragon. An International Variety Entertainment. This included
	Devil's Bridge by Henri Gheon
	To be Quite Frank by Micheál Mac Liammóir
	Two Gentlemen of Soho by A. P. Herbert
	Turkey and Bones and Eating and We Liked It by Gertrude Stein

At the Gaiety Theatre

February 1941	**Dancing Shadow** by Micheál Mac Liammóir
	First Production.
	Ladies in Retirement by Reginald Denham and Edward Percy
March	**Thunder Rock** by Robert Ardrey
	The Forced Marriage by David Sears
April	**Hamlet** (in modern dress) by William Shakespeare
October	**No Time For Comedy** by S. N. Berman
November	**Caesar and Cleopatra** by Bernard Shaw
December	**Quality Street** by J. M. Barrie

At the Gate Theatre

December 1941   **Harlequinade.** An International Variety Entertainment. This included
       Buttery Blondes by Micheál Mac Liammóir
       Red Peppers by Noël Coward
       The Stranger by August Strindberg
       The Marriage, adapted by Lady Gregory from **An Posadh** by Douglas Hyde
       The Old Sailor by A. A. Milne
       A season in Cork followed

At the Gaiety Theatre

March 1942   **Blithe Spirit** by Noël Coward
The Doctor's Boy by Frank Carney
The Light of Heart by Emlyn Williams
       In April 1942 the Company presented a recital by Dame Sybil Thorndike and Sir Lewis Casson at the Gaiety Theatre and the Opera House, Cork.

May   **Summer Harlequinade.** An International Variety Entertainment. This included
       The Tell-tale Heart by Edgar Allan Poe
       The King of the Great Clock Tower by W. B. Yeats, with music by Tyrell Pine
       The Oak Room Mystery by Elmer Rice

October   **The Beggars Opera** by John Gay
Love on the Dole by Walter Greenwood
The Emperor Jones by Eugene O'Neill
The Man of Destiny by Bernard Shaw
       Revived in 1955.
The Man Who Came to Dinner by Kaufman and Hart
       Revived in 1943 and 1946, and on tour.

November   **The Barrel Organ** by Robert Collis
       First Production.
Parnell by Elsie Schauffler

At the Gate Theatre

December 1942   **Jack-in-the-Box.** An International Variety Entertainment. This included
       The Little Match Girl by Hans Christian Andersen
       Thirst by Myles na gCopaleen
       La Sainte Courtisane by Oscar Wilde
       The Fall, edited from **Henry VIII** by William Shakespeare

At the Gaiety Theatre

March 1943   **Anthony and Cleopatra** by William Shakespeare
The Insect Play by the Brothers Capek, adapted by Myles na gCopaleen
The Barretts of Wimpole Street by Rudolf Besier

April   **Ghosts** by Henrik Ibsen
       This production starred Dame Sybil Thorndike and Micheál Mac Liammóir
Captain Brassbound's Conversion
       This production starred Dame Sybil Thorndike and Hilton Edwards.

September   **The Constant Nymph** by Margaret Kennedy
       This Gaiety season also included four revivals

	At the Gate Theatre
November 1943	**Abraham Lincoln** by John Drinkwater
December	**Masquerade.** A Christmas Entertainment. This included

> **Last Tram to Dalkey** by Micheál Mac Liammóir. Lyric and music by Tyrrell Pine
> **The Last Wife** (Catherine Parr) by Maurice Baring. Lyric by Henry VIII
> **The Cask of Amontillado,** adapted by Hilton Edwards from Edgar Allan Poe
> **Exit Harlequin,** adapted from Nickolas Evreinov
> **The Ghost of Abel.** A vision by William Blake. Music by Tyrrell Pine.
> **A la Crepe Suzette** by Micheál Mac Liammóir. Lyric and music by Tyrrell Pine

February 1944	**Desire Under the Elms** by Eugene O'Neill
March	**Jane Eyre,** adapted from Charlotte Brontë by Micheál Mac Liammóir
	First Production. Revived in 1944, and on tour.
May	**Guardian Angel** by M. J. Farrell
	Mr. Bolfry by James Bridie

	At the Gaiety Theatre
September 1944	**Arsenic and Old Lace** by Joseph Kesserling

	At the Gate Theatre
December 1944	**Punchbowl.** A Christmas Entertainment. This included

> **The Happy Journey to Trenton and Camden** by Thorton Wilder
> **The Importance of Being Pussy** by Micheál Mac Liammóir
> Excerpts from **Richard II** by William Shakespeare
> **Reformation, or The Drunkard's Child,** freely adapted by Hilton Edwards from **Ten Nights in a Bar-Room**
> **High Water in Drimnagh** by Christopher Casson
> **Portrait of a Woman with Red Hair** by Micheál Mac Liammóir
> **The Christmas Carol,** adapted by Hilton Edwards from Charles Dickens

	At the Gaiety Theatre
February 1945	**The Picture of Dorian Gray,** adapted from Oscar Wilde by Micheál Mac Liammóir
	First Production. Revived in 1956.
March	**Uncle Harry** by Thomas Job

> In May the Company presented the Théâtre Molière des Londres in **La Malade Imaginaire** at the Gate Theatre.
> In June the Company toured in Northern Ireland under the ausipces of CEMA, with **Where Stars Walk, Othello** and **A Hundred Years Old.**

September	**A Tale of Two Cities,** adapted from Charles Dickens by Micheál Mac Liammóir
	First Production.
November	**The Skin of Our Teeth** by Thornton Wilder
December	**Watch on the Rhine** by Lillian Hellman

	At the Gate Theatre
December 1945	**Prunella** by Laurence Houseman and Granville Barker

	At the Gaiety Theatre
May 1946	**The Merchant of Venice** by William Shakespeare
	A New Production.
	Ill Met by Moonlight by Micheál Mac Liammóir
	First Production. Revived in 1946, 1947, 1948, 1949 and 1969.

	At the Gate Theatre
June 1946	**Duet for Two Hands** by Mary Hayley Bell

	At the Gaiety Theatre
August 1946	**And Pastures New . . .** An International Variety Entertainment.
September	**Trilby** by George du Maurier

October 1946	**Oedipus, the Tyrant,** adapted from Sophocles by the Earl of Longford.
	Portrait of Miriam by Micheál Mac Liammóir
	First Production.
	John Bull's Other Island by Bernard Shaw
	First Production by the Company.

Between November 1947 and February 1948 the Company toured to Belfast, Glasgow, London, Canada and New York. Plays presented on this tour were: **The Old Lady Says 'No', Where Stars Walk, John Bull's Other Island** and, in Canada only, **Portrait of Miriam.**

September 1948	**Abdication** by H. T. Porter-Lowe
	The Mountains Look Different by Micheál Mac Liammóir
	First Production. Transferred to the Gate Theatre.

At the Gate Theatre

February 1949	**The Father** by August Strindberg

At the Gaiety Theatre

March 1949	**To Live In Peace** by G. Forzano

A season at the Opera House, Belfast, followed. Afterwards, during a season in Germany and France with Orson Welles and Ertha Kitt, the events described by Micheál Mac Liammóir in **Each Actor on His Ass** took place.

At the Gate Theatre

December 1950	**Home for Christmas** by Micheál Mac Liammóir
	First Production. Revived in 1976.
February 1951	**The Old Ladies** by Rodney Ackland and Hugh Walpole

At the Gaiety Theatre

February 1951	**Richard II** by William Shakespeare
March	**Liffey Lane** by Maura Laverty
	First Production. Revived in 1951, 1954 and 1955.
April	**Death of a Salesman** by Arthur Miller
May	**The Director** by L. A. G. Strong
October	**Tolka Row** by Maura Laverty
	First Production. Revived in 1951, 1952 and 1954.

At the Gate Theatre

December 1951	**God's Gentry** by Donagh MacDonagh
	First Production.

At the Gaiety Theatre

March 1952	**His Excellency** by Dorothy and Campbell Christie
	Ninotchka by Melchoir Lengyel

A revival of **Hamlet** was presented at the Opera House, Cork, for one week in May, prior to its presentation at Elsinore later in the month, and at the Olympia Theatre, Dublin, for a week following the Danish presentation.

September	**Darkness at Noon** by Arthur Koestler
October	**A Tree in the Crescent** by Maura Laverty
	First Production.

At the Gate Theatre

December	**Ring Round the Moon** by Jean Anouilh
	Revived in the 1955–1956 and the 1975–1976 seasons.
April 1953	**A Sleep of Prisoners** by Christopher Fry
	The Countess Cathleen by W. B. Yeats
June	**An Apple a Day** (**Doctor Knock**) by James Bridie

At the Gaiety Theatre

September 1953	**The Love of Four Colonels** by Peter Ustinov

At the Gate Theatre

December 1953   **Saint Joan** by Bernard Shaw
Revived in 1953 and 1959, and on tour.

At the Gaiety Theatre

June 1954   **The Demon Lover** by Lennox Robinson

At the Gate Theatre

December 1954   **A Slipper for the Moon** by Micheál Mac Liammóir
First Production. Tour in 1955.

March 1955   **Henry IV** by Luigi Pirandello

July 1955   In July Micheál Mac Liammóir starred with Eithne Dunne in **The Mad Woman of Chaillot** by Jean Giradoux. The production was produced and directed at the Olympia Theatre by Joseph Albericci, by arrangement with Illsley and McCabe.

At the Gate Theatre

October 1955   **The Lark** by Jean Anouilh
Tour in 1956.

The Lark was followed by revivals of five plays. In February 1956 the Company toured to Egypt and Malta. The plays presented on this tour were: **The Lark, The Merchant of Venice, Ring Round the Moon, The Man of Destiny, The Seagull, Oedipus the King, The Picture of Dorian Gray.**

In August and September 1956 Micheál Mac Liammóir played with Jimmy O'Dea in **Gateway to Gaiety** and in September he played in **The Wayward Saint**, presented by the Globe Theatre at the Gaiety and directed by Hilton Edwards. From December 1956 to February 1957 Micheál Mac Liammóir played in **Cinderella**, again with Jimmy O'Dea, at the Gaiety. In August Micheál Mac Liammóir appeared in Jonathan Griffin's **The Hidden King** at the Edinburgh Festival.

At the Gaiety Theatre

February 1957   **Julius Caesar** by William Shakespeare
Revival, in modern dress.

March   **Step in the Hollow** by Donagh Mac Donagh
First Production.

Anastasia by Marcel Maurette, adapted by Guy Bolton

In May 1957 Micheál Mac Liammóir played in **The Pageant of Saint Patrick**, with Anew MacMaster in the title role. Hilton Edwards directed the pageant, which was presented at Croke Park.

Following the An Tostal production of **The Old Lady Says 'No'** with Micheál Mac Liammóir and Iris Lawler at the Gate, presented by Longford Productions and directed by Hilton Edwards, the theatre was closed for alterations from July 1957 to January 1958.

At the Olympia Theatre

November 1958   **The Informer**, adapted from Liam O'Flaherty by Micheál Mac Liammóir
First Production.

At the Gaiety Theatre

April 1959   **Mother Courage** by Berthold Brecht

Micheál Mac Liammóir played in Sir John Gielgud's production of Shakespeare's **Much Ado About Nothing**, starring Sir John and Margaret Leighton. It opened in Boston, August 1959, and in New York in November.

At the Opera House, Belfast

February 1960   **Chimes at Midnight**, compiled by Orson Welles from Shakespeare's plays and Holinshed's Chronicle. This production, which starred Orson Welles, transferred to the Gaiety Theatre, Dublin.

September 1960	**The Importance of Being Oscar** by Oscar Wilde and Micheál Mac Liammóir *First Production. Revived many times.* Although the official first night was 19 September at the Gaiety, a full try-out performance had been given three nights earlier at the Gaelic Hall, Curragh Camp. Between mid-October and Christmas 1960, Micheál Mac Liammóir played **The Importance of Being Oscar** in London, Brighton and Cambridge. In January 1961 he played it at the Royal Court Theatre, London; in March he opened at the Lyceum, New York, and that summer he toured the production in South America.
September 1961	**Saint Joan of the Stockyards** by Berthold Brecht *Transferred to the Olympia Theatre.* Between September 1961 and March 1963 Micheál Mac Liammóir toured extensively in **The Importance of Being Oscar.** At this time Hilton Edwards was Head of Drama at Radio Telefís Eireann. In September 1962 Micheál Mac Liammóir appeared as Iago opposite William Marshall's Othello in Hilton Edwards's production of Shakespeare's play at the Gaiety Theatre. The production, a Dublin Theatre Festival presentation, transferred to the Continent for two weeks.
April 1963	**I Must be Talking to my Friends** by Micheál Mac Liammóir and others *First Production. Revived many times.* In May, **I Must be Talking to my Friends**, with a revival of **The Importance of Being Oscar,** transferred to the Aldwych Theatre, London.
	At the Opera House, Belfast
June 1963	**The Evangelist** by Sam Thompson *First Production. Transferred to the Gaiety Theatre, Dublin.*
	At the Gaiety Theatre
September 1963	**The Last P.M.** by Conor Farrington *First Production.*
October	**The Aspern Papers**, adapted from Henry James by Michael Redgrave **The Roses Are Real** by Patrick Patterson *First Production. Transferred to London.* From March to August 1963 Micheál Mac Liammóir toured in Australia and New Zealand.
September 1964	**Philadelphia, Here I Come!** by Brian Friel *First Production. Revivals in 1965 and 1968.*
	At the Gate Theatre
September 1964	**You Never Can Tell** by Bernard Shaw
October	**The Bernard Shaw Story** by Bernard Shaw and Bramwell Fletcher
	At the Gaiety Theatre
April 1965	**Rashomon**, adapted from the Japanese of Ryonosuke Akutagann by Fay and Michael Kanin
	At the Shelbourne Hotel, Dublin
June 1965	**Talking About Yeats** by W. B. Yeats and Micheál Mac Liammóir *First Production. Many revivals.* From October to December 1965 Micheál Mac Liammóir toured **The Importance of Being Oscar** in Scandinavia and England. The Edwards–Mac Liammóir production of **Philadelphia, Here I come!** by Brian Friel transferred to Philadelphia and Boston, and opened in New York in February 1966.
	At the Gate Theatre
July 1967	**Lovers** by Brian Friel *First Production. Transferred to Los Angeles and New York in 1968.*

1968   At the Gaiety Theatre
        Crystal and Fox by Brian Friel
            First Production. Transferred to the Gate Theatre.

        At the Gate Theatre
February 1969   **Rosencrantz and Guildenstern are Dead** by Tom Stoppard
March   **The Promise** by Alexsei Arbuzov
                In August 1969 Micheál Mac Liammóir appeared at the Abbey Theatre
                in the title role of **Swift** by Eugene McCabe, directed by Sir Tyrone
                Guthrie.
October   **King Herod Explains** by Conor Cruise O'Brien
                    First Production. Screened on RTE Television.
                 The Liar by Micheál Mac Liammóir
                Following the production of **King Herod Explains** and **The Liar**, which
                closed on 25 October 1969, Micheál Mac Liammóir's seventieth birthday,
                the Gate Theatre was closed for renovations. It reopened on 15 March
                1971.

        1971 Season
March 1971   **It's Later Than You Think (M. Ornifle)** by Jean Anouilh
                The run of this production was terminated due to the illness of Micheál
                Mac Liammóir. During March and April the Company presented Marie
                Kean in **Soft Morning, City** and Robert Bernal in **Mr. Joyce is Leaving
                Paris.** These productions were followed by revivals of **Heartbreak House,
                The Importance of Being Oscar** and **Romeo and Juliet.**
                During June the Company presented Bill Golding and Louise Studley in
                Go Where Glory Waits Thee.
June   **The Signalman's Apprentice** by Brian Phelan
                *First Irish Production. The last production in which Hilton Edwards and
                Micheál Mac Liammóir appeared together.*
July   **Slow Dance on the Killing Ground** by William Hanley
                First Irish Production.
                The Edwards – Mac Liammóir season ended in September 1971.

        Dublin Theatre Festival 1972
March   **The True Story of the Horrid Popish Plot** by Desomnd Forristal
                First Production. Revived in 1975.
             The Samson Riddle by Wolf Mankowitz
                First Production.

        1972–1973
March 1973   **The Servant of Two Masters** by Carlo Goldoni
April   **After Sunset** by Terence de Vere White
                First Production.
                The Edwards – Mac Liammóir Season ended in May 1973.

        1973–1974 Season
September 1973   **Noone** by Joe O'Donnell
                    First Production, in association with Gemini Productions.
October   **Prelude in Kazbek Street** by Micheál Mac Liammóir
                    First Production.
April 1974   **Black Man's Country** by Desmond Forristal
                    First Production. Revived in October 1974.

                The Edwards – Mac Liammóir Season ended in June 1974.

1974–1975 Season

October 1974	**The Voice of Shem**, adapted by Mary Manning from James Joyce
	The Company presented Eamon Morrissey in **The Brother** *in December.*
December	**The Good-Natured Man** by Oliver Goldsmith
	This was the last play in which Micheál Mac Liammóir appeared.
March 1975	**Miss Julie** by August Strindberg
	The Edwards – Mac Liammóir Season ended in June 1975.

1975–1976 Season

October 1975	**The Real Charlotte**, adapted by Terence de Vere White and Adrian Vale from Somerville and Ross.
	First Production.
	In December Micheál Mac Liammóir gave six performances of **The Importance of Being Oscar.** This was his last appearance on stage.
February 1976	**The Doctor's Dilemma** by Bernard Shaw
May	**The Seventh Sin** by Desmond Forristal
	First Production. Revived in October 1976.
	The Edwards – Mac Liammóir Season ended in June 1976.

1976–1977 Season

February 1977	**The Devil's Disciple** by Bernard Shaw
May	**Equus** by Peter Shaffer
	First Irish Production. Revived in December 1977, when it ran until the Edwards – Mac Liammóir Season ended in July 1977.

1977–1978 Season

| November 1977 | **Major Barbara** by Bernard Shaw |

Micheál Mac Liammóir died in Dublin on 6 March 1978.

The Company will return to the Gate on 3 October 1978 with the First Production of **Proxopera**, adapted by Peter Luke from the novel by Benedict Kiely

A commemorative exhibition of the Company's work 1928–1978, **All for Hecuba**, will open at the Municipal Gallery of Modern Art, Dublin, on 4 October 1978.

DIRECTION

Hilton Edwards directed all but fourteen of the above Edwards – Mac Liammóir productions. The directors of these fourteen plays were :
Micheál Mac Liammóir (**Wife to a Famous Man, The Terrible Meek, No Time for Comedy** and the 1969 revival of **Ill Met By Moonlight**); William Sherwood (**The Mollusc**); Denis Johnston (**Happy Family**); Shelah Richards (**Magic**); Reginald Jarman (**Judgement Day**); Peter Letts (**Ninotchka.** He also jointly directed **Death of a Salesman** with Hilton Edwards); Chloe Gibson (**You Never Can Tell** and **The Signalman's Apprentice**); James Murphy (**The Aspern Papers**); Alan Richardson (the 1973 revival of **The Stronger**); Louis Lentin (**Slow Dance on the Killing Ground** and **The Voice of Shem**) and Christopher Casson (**The Doctor's Dilemma, The Devil's Disciple** and **Major Barbara**).